MEN-AT-ARMS SERIES

EDITOR: MARTIN WINDROW

Wellington's Specialist Troops

Text *by* PHILIP HAYTHORNTHWAITE

Colour plates by BRYAN FOSTEN

OSPREY PUBLISHING LONDON

Published in 1988 by
Osprey Publishing Ltd
59 Grosvenor Street, London, W1X 9DA
© Copyright 1988 Osprey Publishing Ltd

British Library Cataloguing in Publication Data

Haythornthwaite, Philip J. (Philip John), *1951* –
Wellington's specialist troops. – (Men-
at-arms series; V.204).
1. British. Special Forces. Uniforms, 1790–
1830
I. Title   II. Fosten, Bryan   III. Series
355.1′4′0941

ISBN 0-85045-862-5

Filmset in Great Britain
Printed through Bookbuilders Ltd, Hong Kong

Artist's note

Readers may care to note that the original paintings
from which the colour plates in this book were
prepared are available for private sale. All
reproduction copyright whatsoever is retained by the
publisher. All enquiries should be addressed to:

Bryan Fosten
5 Ross Close
Nyetimber
Nr. Bognor Regis
Sussex PO21 3JW

The publishers regret that they can enter into no
correspondence upon this matter.

Introduction

Excluding the various Staff departments, the 'specialist' elements of the British Army of the Napoleonic Wars may be divided into four sections: artillery, engineers, transport and commissariat, and medical. The two senior corps, the Royal Artillery and the engineer services, were not strictly part of the army but came under the direction of the Master-General of Ordnance, rather than the Commander-in-Chief and the Horse Guards. Thus, these two branches had greatly different characteristics, most notably in the level of training given their officers, whose promotion was by seniority and not, as in the infantry and cavalry, partly dependent upon the system of purchase of commissions.

The Royal Artillery

Compared with the vast numbers of cannon employed by other European armies, Britain's artillery arm was small, despite the expansion which occurred throughout the Napoleonic Wars (there were only 274 artillery officers in 1791, rising to 727 in 1814). The corps headquarters at Woolwich, where the artillery depot and academy were situated, was controlled by the Deputy Adjutant-General, Royal Artillery, whose staff of one assistant and five clerks ('of whom four are merely sergeants') amazingly ran the entire artillery establishment. Consequently, the Royal Artillery resembled a large family, close-knit and justifiably proud of its professional competence—an attitude which tended to distance artillery officers from those of other services. The necessity that all officers be highly trained meant that no immediate expansions could be effected, a factor which

inhibited the effectiveness of the artillery until such time as Woolwich could produce trained gunnery officers. The initial shortage led to the retention of 'battalion guns' (see below) long after they had been recognised as outmoded.

There is little space here to detail the ordnance employed during the Napoleonic Wars; reference should be made to *Artillery Equipments of the Napoleonic Wars* (T. Wise, Men-at-Arms 96, London

Officer, Royal Artillery: a print in the *British Military Library* series published by J. Carpenter & Co., January 1799, showing the uniform worn during the bulk of the Napoleonic Wars — dark blue with scarlet facings, gilt buttons, gold epaulette and hat-decorations, crimson sash, white breeches and black boots.

Corporal (left) and gunners, Royal Artillery, 1806: a print by John A. Atkinson, published by Miller and Walker in January 1807, from Atkinson's *Picturesque Representation of the ... Costumes of Great Britain*. The corporal wears blue breeches with yellow lace, and the two gunners have horns on scarlet cords. All wear yellow tufts on the shoulder straps, but note that there appear to be insufficient loops on the jacket breast. The cartridge box badge appears to be the older crown-on-scroll variety.

1979). In 1803 the Royal Artillery consisted of eight battalions, each of ten companies; a 9th battalion was formed in 1806 and a 10th in 1808. Battalions did not serve in the field as complete units, but were employed in company-sized 'brigades', each including a detachment of artillery drivers, who although belonging to a separate organisation (see below) became part of the brigade to which they were attached. (Prior to 1802, guns were grouped for administrative purposes into 'brigades' of about 12 pieces.) The term 'battery'—a 'brigade' normally of six guns—was usually employed to describe a gun-position rather than in the modern sense. Establishment of a 'brigade' or company in 1808 was officially two captains, two 1st lieutenants, one 2nd lieutenant, four sergeants, four corporals, nine bombardiers, three drummers and 116 gunners. Each 'brigade' of Foot Artillery (a title sometimes used to differentiate the ordinary field

artillery from the mounted horse 'brigades') normally had six pieces of artillery, usually five guns and one howitzer, though all-gun units, and occasionally all-howitzer, were not unknown. In addition to the six pieces and their limbers, each 'brigade' possessed eight ammunition-waggons, three baggage-waggons, a spare-wheel waggon and a field forge, with 200 draught animals and about 100 drivers. There were also more specialist artillery vehicles for the transportation of siege-artillery, mortars and the like.

The variety of ordnance used was immense: Adye's *Bombardier and Pocket Gunner* (London, 2nd edn. 1802), the artillerist's *vade mecum* of the period, lists no less than 64 distinct types of ordnance (including mortars), though only about ten of these were in common use for field service. For the field batteries the 'light 6-pdr.' and the $5\frac{1}{2}$-in. howitzer were the standard weapons; after failing in the Peninsular War, the original 8- and 10-in. howitzers were withdrawn, the $5\frac{1}{2}$-in. and $4\frac{2}{5}$-in. remaining in use. Eventually the 6-pdr. was replaced in the 'foot' brigades with the vastly superior 9-pdr., but the 6-pdr. remained in use as a horse artillery gun. Guns were normally made of 'brass' (actually bronze), though iron guns (less prone to distortion when hot) were employed for siege-work.

The process of increasing the weight and quantity of artillery was slow, and the number never sufficient; for example, in May 1809 the British and King's German Legion artillery in the Peninsula consisted of only three batteries of light 6-pdrs. and three of 3-pdrs., the latter of very limited hitting-power. By the Vittoria campaign the strength had increased to seven brigades of 9-pdrs. two of heavy 6-pdrs. and four of light 6-pdrs. By Waterloo, all the foot brigades had five 9-pdrs. and one $5\frac{1}{2}$-in. howitzer.

The Horse Artillery was formed in 1793 as support for cavalry, all gunners either mounted or riding upon battery vehicles. In 1801 there were seven troops (or 'brigades') of Royal Horse Artillery, rising to 12 by 1806. Troop-establishment in 1808 was: one captain, one second-captain, three lieutenants, two staff sergeants, three sergeants, three corporals, six bombardiers, 80 gunners, 60 drivers, one farrier, one carriage-smith, two shoeing-smiths, two collar-makers, one wheelwright and one trumpeter. As in the Foot Artillery ctual strength fluctuated; Mercer's 'G' Troop in 1815, for example, included a surgeon, 80 gunners and 84 drivers. Mercer's equipment included the following vehicles:

Five 9-pdrs. and one $5\frac{1}{2}$-in. howitzer, eight horses each: 48 horses

Nine ammunition-waggons (one per gun plus one spare per 'division'), six horses each: 54 horses

Forge, curricle-cart, baggage-waggon, four horses each: 12 horses

Spare-wheel cart: 6 horses

Six mounted detachments, eight horses each: 48 horses

Mounts of two staff sergeants, collar-makers and farrier: 5 horses

Officers' horses (property of Board of Ordnance): 6 horses

Officers' horses (personally owned, two per officer, one for surgeon): 11 horses

Officers' baggage mules: 6

Spare horses: 30

The troop was split into three 'divisions' of two 'subdivisions' each; each subdivision consisted of one gun, one ammunition-waggon and a gun-crew. Each division was commanded by a lieutenant, each right subdivision by a sergeant and each left subdivision by a corporal. The troop could also be divided into two 'half-brigades' of three sub-divisions each, one half-brigade commanded by the captain and one by the second-captain. The practice of guns operating in divisions (i.e. pairs) was standard throughout the period. Horses were not always used; in 1809 Alexander Dickson reported one brigade 'chiefly drawn by the fine carriage mules of Lisbon'. Foot companies were generally known by the name of their commander (e.g. 'Geary's Company') and horse brigades either by this method or by their designation-letter, e.g. 'A Troop'.

Heavier guns were used in defence of for-ifications and with the siege train. The commonest siege guns were 24- and 18-pdrs., but even more cumbersome pieces were employed, 42- and 32-pdrs., in both brass and iron, and prior to Ciudad Rodrigo the army in the Peninsula had to rely on a veritable museum of Spanish and Portuguese ordnance dating back to the 1620s, with no standard calibre and limited effect. Siege-craft was greatly hindered by insufficient matériel and lack of trained engineers, and even when Wellington was reinforced prior to the second siege of Badajoz, he received Russian 18-pdrs. which his ammunition did not fit! Latterly, naval guns and crews were landed in Spain, which were a considerable improvement. The siege-train was ponderous in the extreme, relying upon eight pairs of bullocks per gun for transportation, with ammunition dragged in ox-carts. Mortars, used exclusively for sieges, were generally even more immobile, transported on flat-bed carts from which they had to be unloaded by triangle gin and block and tackle (the 13-in. iron mortar, 3 ft $7\frac{1}{2}$ in. long, weighed 4,032 lbs).

Other ordnance operated by the Royal Artillery included a mountain battery formed for the crossing of the Pyrenees, equipped with six 3-pdrs. which were broken down for transportation on mule-back, and crewed by a mixture of British and Portuguese gunners; and the two Rocket Troops, officially established as separate entities in January 1813.

The most mobile of 'artillery', the 172 men of a Rocket Troop could carry (without vehicles) 840 missiles; but though their effect on enemy morale could be profound, accuracy was so limited that their potential was never realised. 40,000 Congreve rockets were fired at Copenhagen; yet though the Rocket Troops served in Spain, at Leipzig, New Orleans and Waterloo, Wellington was continually hostile, accepting a troop in the Peninsula simply 'to get the horses ... I do not wish to set fire to any town, and I do not know any other use for rockets'. The rocketeers were initially sent on active service almost untrained; as Col. Frazer wrote, 'I had to manage the medley called the rocket troop, composed of men hastily scraped together, utterly ignorant of the arm they are to use, the rockets equipped in five varieties of manner and liable to as many mistakes'. At Waterloo the Rocket Troop also had 6-pdr. guns.

The higher command of the Royal Artillery often did not match the excellence of the officers and gunners. Until 1813 Wellington possessed no satisfactory artillery commander; of one (Howarth) he wrote, 'I will be lucky if he does not get me into a scrape', and even his own brigade-major thought him 'excessively irritable ... neither confidence in himself or anyone else'. Another, William Borthwick, was told by Wellington that he 'wanted an active officer to fill so important a situation as chief of artillery' and was recommended to go home! In 1813 Wellington at last found a competent artillery chief when he appointed Alexander Dickson on the strength of his Por-

Gunners, Royal Artillery: aquatint by I. C. Stadler after Charles Hamilton Smith, from the latter's *Costume of the Army of the British Empire*, published 1 February 1815. Note that no tufts are worn on the shoulder straps; one gunner in this version has red turnbacks, one white. The cartridge box bears the later crowned-strap badge with 'GR' in the centre, and one carries the distinctive Foot Artillery sword. Unusually, the shako-cords extend around the rear of the cap.

tuguese commission, when there were seven RA officers with the army who were his regimental seniors. Dickson invariably wore Portuguese uniform to avoid giving offence!

The organisation of the Portuguese and King's German Legion artillery was on British lines; the KGL, for example, had three foot brigades and two horse troops.

Transportation of artillery was the responsibility of the Corps of Drivers, alias 'Wee Gees', which, like the RHA was the creation of the Duke of Richmond, and was perhaps his most important contribution to British military progress. Previously, artillery teams and drivers had been hired from civilian contractors who remained outside the army—a thoroughly unsatisfactory system the evils of which were demonstrated at Fontenoy, when hired Flemish drivers and horses fled, leaving the gunners unable to save their cannon. Despite this, it took a further 49 years before the system was altered and the Corps of Drivers formed in 1794, though the contracting of civilians appears to have continued for some time after that. In practice, however, the Corps of Drivers was one of the worst elements in the army.

The earnest Dickson described the corps as an 'Augean stable': 'Many of the officers are negligent and indifferent to their duty ... constantly giving their names in sick and in several cases absenting themselves without leave'. Worse, the officers neglected their men, leaving them unpaid for months and even years, even appropriating the funds to their own use. In 1808 the Corps consisted of eight troops, each of 554 men (450 of whom were drivers, in five sections of 90, plus assorted craftsmen), 945 draught horses and 75 riding horses, commanded by a captain. Ultimately there were 11 troops. These troops were divided among the artillery companies, so that little supervision by their own officers was possible, resulting in poor discipline and morale. As noted in 1813, 'They want from the nature of their duty, dispersed in fractional parts, more superintendence than any corps, and yet ... they have not a field officer or superintending power belonging to them'. Notorious above most other corps, they were described by Swabey of the RHA as 'that nest of infamy', whose activities extended to stealing ammunition and selling it to the Portuguese army. Only

Royal Artillery officer, *c.* 1815 or slightly later: an unpublished contemporary sketch showing the scarlet lapels with pointed gold lace loops, which have a very marked scarlet 'light' in the centre.

complete integration with the artillery could have solved the problem, but this was not undertaken until after the war. Not surprisingly, there was considerable conflict between the artillerymen and the Corps of Drivers.

Uniforms

Royal Artillery

The uniform of the Royal Artillery was always styled upon that of the Line infantry, the coat blue with red facings and yellow lace. At the beginning of the Revolutionary Wars the uniform was as shown in Plate A2: the dark blue coat had scarlet lapels, cuffs and standing collar, with square-ended yellow lace loops and the white turnbacks prescribed in

1782; black bicorn with yellow lace binding and white plume, white breeches and black gaiters. Equipment was as described for Plate A2, with all leatherwork white (including cartridge box) as ordered from June 1772, and the knapsack of painted canvas. (Some sources for this period indicate red turnbacks; but these, as well as blue breeches and waistcoats, were the distinctive uniform of the RA Invalid Battalion.) Buttons bore the Ordnance arms (a shield bearing three roundshot over three cannon), in pewter for the rank and file; the Royal Irish Artillery (which merged with the RA in 1801) wore a similar pattern but with two cannon balls over a harp over a gun, with or without unit-title. For working dress, according to an order of September 1790, each gunner was provided with '1 check shirt, 1 canvas frock, 1 canvas trowsers, 1 leather cap'. Similar uniforms were described as the issue for recruits, plus a 'blue cloth jacket' which in 1794 cost 9s. 8d. 'Worsted gloves the battalion pattern' are mentioned in a Woolwich garrison order of 19 November 1794.

By 1794 the bicorn had been replaced for active service by a black 'round hat', which appears in contemporary pictures in a number of shapes, some squat and symmetrical, others conical, with flat or curled brim. Described as a 'Mother Shipton' by Mercer (after the renowned Yorkshire witch), the hat had a broad yellow lace band around the base and a cockade at the front, below a scarlet tuft. White hats for service in the West Indies were proposed in October 1791. Mercer describes the brim as 'very narrow', but some sources show wider ones, some with a yellow lace loop for the cockade as mentioned in the proposal for the white hat; 'gold button and loop and cockade to be placed in the front of the crown'. A statement that the 'Mother Shipton' continued in use until 1813 which has been repeated in several modern works is undoubtedly in error, caused by a misinterpretation of the 1813 order which discontinued the 'cap of sugar-loaf shape' which obviously refers to the 'stovepipe' shako. The 'Mother Shipton' seems actually to have been discontinued in 1796–97, an order of 17 April 1796 stating that 'the Men are to have cocked hats, and that the Officers are to have plain cocked hats, as formerly in use', which at Woolwich were to be

Foot Artillery at Waterloo: etching by S. Mitan after Capt. George Jones, 1816. The officer wears plastron lapels and a curved sabre from a waist belt; note the sword worn by one gunner.

provided by 4 June 1796—confirming Mercer's belief that the bicorn was again in use by the end of 1797. The bicorn worn at this time was larger than that in use before, and is shown in Scott's series of prints to be without lace, but with a white tuft. For the Royal Irish Artillery the hat-lace was apparently removed in 1798.

Officers' uniforms resembled those of the men, with a crimson waist-sash, gilt buttons and without lace; Edward Dayes shows the hat unadorned but for a cockade and white feather. Dayes shows a gold epaulette on the right shoulder, and as early as 5 July 1791 a system of rank-marking was instituted: 'Field Officers to be distinguished by . . . wearing an epaulette on each shoulder'. Other items are described in an order of 8 August 1794: 'The Officers lately appointed are informed, that the regimental waistcoats are without flaps, and with one row of buttons only, the same as the Men's. The breeches, which are cloth or kerseymere, are likewise the same as the Men's, and buckle at the knee. The tops of the boots are bound and lined with white leather, and buckle up with a black strap. The sword has a straight blade, and the length of it as established by His Majesty's regulations; it is to be worn with a crimson and gold sword knot. The lappels of the coat are buttoned back, and hooked together, and the skirts hooked up'.

To match the 'Mother Shipton' hats of the rank-and-file, officers also adopted 'round hats', somewhat lower-crowned and with wider brims curled at the sides, with two varieties of decoration, both shown by De Loutherberg in his 1794 paintings. One variety has a gold band, brim-edge and cockade-loop like that of the men, and is apparently that described in May 1795: '. . . the uniform to be worn by a Deputy Adjutant General attached to the Artillery, is to be blue, with a scarlet lappell, cuffs, and collar, and the button holes to be gold, with gold epaulettes, one on each shoulder. A plain hat, with gold button, loop and band round it. White waistcoat, and breeches'.

The other variety is shown in Plate A1, with a black bearskin crest, a large black cockade at the left and three lines of gold cord encircling the crown; this is shown in several portraits, most notably that of Sir William Congreve by De Loutherberg, which also depicts the coat with the lapels half closed, and

The Ordnance arms: the standard design, upon an officer's flat, gilt button.

the collar a stand-and-fall pattern with a button at the front corner. Also shown at the time are long trousers instead of the usual breeches and boots. De Loutherberg shows an officer wearing the bicorn instead of the 'round hat', and also depicts a white cloth forage cap shaped similarly to that in Plate F3, with blue piping around the edges and apparently bearing 'RA' on the front.

In accordance with the new infantry pattern, the uniform changed around 1796; the lapels were made to fasten to the waist, but in 1797 they were removed and the rank-and-file coat became a single-breasted jacket. The closed-lapel version of brief duration may have been worn by the Royal Artillery, for a drawing of 1800 shows a horse artilleryman wearing such scarlet lapels, an unusual but not impossible uniform. Probably at this date the other ranks' yellow lace changed to 'bastion' shape, though the statement that only five loops were worn on the breast is presumably taken from Atkinson's illustration which is almost certainly in error. Officers' coats were double-breasted with standing collar, and closed to the waist; Mercer notes that the lapels could be buttoned over but were more usually worn with 'the three upper buttons undone and the lapels turned back, with the cambric shirt-frill pulled out in the form of a

9

An artillery shoulder belt plate with engraved design; one of a number of recorded variations, this is either a battalion's distinctive pattern or belonging to a volunteer corps.

cock's comb. Still no lace, save the epaulet. I remember at Clonmel in 1802 venturing to stick grenades on our skirts'. Eventually turnback ornaments of 'an embroidered true lover's knot on red cloth' were authorized, followed by 'cord lace and embroidery' in the form of button loops. Similar decorations were worn by the Royal Irish Artillery (which ceased to exist in 1801), a recorded coat having gold loops, turnbacks bearing red hearts, pockets with four gold loops and two horizontal loops at the rear waist, and two-inch deep cuffs with four buttons with horizontal loops placed one above the other.

Officers wore a variety of legwear, sanctioned officially in 1803: 'The Master General [of Ordnance] permits Officers of Artillery to wear blue pantaloons and boots in the field; and considering the possibility, at this particular period, of Officers being suddenly called into the field, permits blue pantaloons and boots to be worn in

Garrison, except on guard, under arms, or any dressed parade'. Frederick Robinson, commissioned in 1803, wrote that 'on full dress parades, on guard and on Sundays we wore white leather breeches, with stiff leather boots ... At other times we wore tight blue pantaloons, with Hessian boots over them ... The custom of appearing at Mess in full evening dress . . . in white kerseymere knee-breeches, with white silk stockings, and shoes with large silver or plated buckles on the instep, had nearly gone out of use in the Army except at balls and King's levées . . . on the afternoon undress parades the men appeared in "Laboratory frocks"'.

The officers' sash was the usual crimson net, Robinson describing how 'the netting opened out a considerable width, forming, I may say, a sort of hammock. I wore one of these dimensions which had been my father's. They afterwards became considerably reduced in size'. In 1785 officers wore white stocks, but black became universal shortly after; Mercer describes his as black velvet, 'into which a padded stuffing was introduced to keep it up; or it was worn over a sufficient accumulation of white muslin, on which one-eighth of an inch in breadth was to border the upper edge of the stock as a finish'.

Officers' swords were carried on a waist belt, but in 1779 the 1st and 3rd Bns. had been given permission to use shoulder belts, and from 1796 these were worn by all; an order of 30 October 1796 states that 'The Master General is extremely willing to comply with the wishes of the Colonels Commandant, and desires they will fix upon a cross-belt and plate for the sword, which may be uniform with that worn in the Army'. Extant plates include several designs, but the general pattern (probably worn until 1824) was probably an oval gilt plate with beaded rim, bearing a crowned, blue-enamelled strap with white edges surrounding a red enamel centre bearing a gilt 'GR', the crown with red cap and white 'pearls', the whole backed by an engraved star, with 'ROYAL' above and 'ARTILLERY' below. An oblong brass plate bearing a crown flanked by 'G III' and 'R' above a gun, above '3' and two piles of cannon balls, above 'ROYAL ARTILLERY', was presumably the pre-1796 pattern of the 3rd Battalion. A similar plate is known with the number '4', one specimen bearing the cypher of William IV, so presumably it remained the 4th Bn.'s pattern throughout. Other extant plates bear the Ordnance arms, which may belong to volunteer artillery; or a gun and cannon balls; and one bearing the Ordnance arms with 'ROYAL BRITISH' above and 'ARTILLERY' below on scrolls may have been designed as a distinction from the Royal Irish, pre-1801. Although gunners' belts normally carried pickers and hammer, oval brass plates are recorded bearing the Ordnance shield with 'ROYAL' above and 'ARTILLERY' below.

Officers' swords were originally of the 1786 style (a straight-bladed 'spadroon' with gilt hilt, the exact pattern unregulated and dependent upon personal taste), but in October 1796 General Orders stated that 'The Officers of Artillery are to conform to the uniform hat and sword, as established by His Majesty for the Army', which had to be in use 'before the beginning of Summer, so that the Regiment when assembled may appear uniform'. This was the 1796 infantry sword, used until 1822, which was highly unpopular; Robertson thought it wretched, and Mercer wrote: 'Nothing could be more useless or more ridiculous ... good neither for cut nor thrust, and was a perfect incumbrance. In the Foot Artillery, when away from headquarters, we generally wore dirks instead of it. Generals, and our Field Officers, seemed to wear what they pleased, and after the Egyptian expedition the Mamaluke [sic] sabre was quite the rage'.

As for the infantry, the 'stovepipe' shako was adopted in 1801 (Plates C1 and C2), with a brass plate with asymmetrical sides including an arrowhead-point at the top, with a raised design of 'GR' within a crowned strap inscribed 'ROYAL. REGt. OF. ARTILLERY.' backed by a trophy of arms, with a mortar and two piles of roundshot at the bottom. At the front was a white tuft which in 1805 was ordered not to exceed 10 in., or 13 in. for sergeants and officers; in 1808 it was ordered that there should be no difference in the length of plume between the ranks. Officers continued to wear the bicorn with white plume, though the Prince Regent's wardrobe accounts for late 1811 note a black and red feather for officers of Foot Artillery—conceivably for undress, or an unadopted project.

Some variations in the jacket of the rank and file are noted, some sources showing yellow cuff-edging

Gilt shako plate of 1812 pattern, different from that normally attributed to the Royal Artillery: conceivably a musician's or possible officer's pattern, or one restricted to a particular battalion.

in addition to that edging the collar; turnbacks were laced yellow, and the pockets appear to have carried loops of the usual bastion pattern, and to have been framed with yellow lace. Shoulder straps were red, edged with yellow lace, and at times yellow worsted tufts are shown (for example by Atkinson), though as late as the Hamilton Smith plate of the 1812 uniform untufted straps appear, as they do in Dighton's pictures before that date; conceivably tufts were worn by some battalions and not others. About 1802 the buttons of Ordnance arms design (which carried the number '3' for the 3rd Bn.) were replaced by buttons bearing 'GR' within a crowned strap inscribed 'Royal Regt. of Artillery'. Atkinson shows blue pantaloons with yellow stripe, worn with short black gaiters (Plate C1), perhaps a walking-out uniform or a battalion pattern. For active service, overalls came into use during the Peninsular War, Dighton showing an early example in white with black buttons on the outer seam. Latterly the ordinary grey overalls worn over similar gaiters were adopted for campaign dress.

Equipment remained virtually unchanged, but latterly a different cartridge-box badge is depicted, a brass crowned strap encircling 'GR'; for knapsack decoration, see Plate E3. It has often been assumed that the Foot Artillery sabre (which appears in numerous illustrations up to 1815, worn on a single shoulder belt or in place of the bayonet) was similar to the French *sabre-briquet*, with a slightly curved blade and single-bar brass hilt, even though the illustrations show a much more angular knuckle-bow. The actual weapon was probably that illustrated in Plate C1, having an exceptionally

The unique hilt of the Foot Artillery sabre, *c.* 1800–1816, shown in numerous contemporary illustrations. Brass hilt with ribbed black leather grip; single-edged 25-in. straight blade, extremely thick and heavy.

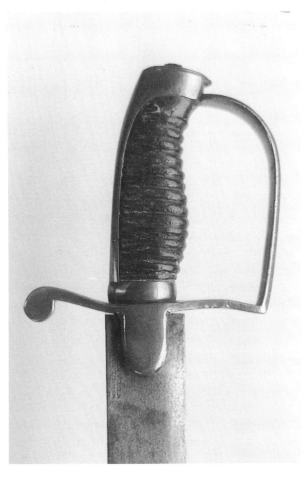

thick, heavy straight blade. Known examples bear makers' marks appropriate to the period from about 1800 (when it is likely that the sword was adopted), and it appears to have been carried by the Royal Artillery until the introduction of the so-called 'Spanish pattern' in about 1816. The musket of the Foot Artillery was like that of the infantry, though a sightly shorter and lighter 'Artillery musket' was in use latterly.

The single epaulettes of officers below field rank were identical until it was ordered that captains were to have a bullion fringe and subalterns coarse cord—a 'shabby distinction' according to Robertson which was soon discontinued, though subalterns' epaulettes henceforth had thinner bullions; presumably in 1810, when the same distinctions were ordered for the infantry. For field officers, silver rank badges were worn on the epaulette strap from this date, a crown and star for colonels, a crown for lieutenant colonels and a star for majors. Corporals and sergeants appear to have had better-quality uniforms than those of gunners (the 1792 prices show considerable differences; £1 0s. 3d for a private, £1 6s. 2d for a bombardier, £1 10s. 2d for a corporal and £2 14s. 1d for a sergeant's coat). In 1788 all had similarly-laced hats, but by 1792 sergeants' hats cost 4s. more than those of the others, implying the use of gold lace. In 1788 corporals were ordered to have two gold lace epaulettes and bombardiers one. By 1799 sergeants and staff sergeants wore gold lace instead of yellow, staff sergeants with two gold bullion epaulettes and sergeants with gold-laced shoulder straps; corporals had two fringed epaulettes and bombardiers one on the right shoulder, probably in yellow.

The 1802 regulations which introduced NCO chevrons did not apply to corps under the aegis of the Board of Ordnance, but the Royal Artillery apparently adopted the system at that date or shortly after, staff sergeants with four gold chevrons and sergeants three, corporals with two yellow and bombardiers one. Initially these were probably sewn directly on to the sleeve, but later were probably set on scarlet backing. In August 1813 a new rank was instituted, 'company sergeant', for which see Plate E2. NCO chevrons were worn on both sleeves by 1815. Sergeants carried spontoons as in the infantry, and doubtless the sergeants' version of the 1796-pattern infantry sword

Sergeants' waist-sashes were apparently crimson, despite a protest in 1796 in which 'his Lordship and the Board [of Ordnance] would rather prefer to be blue and red instead of crimson as proposed'. Greatcoats were of infantry pattern, the officers' variety described in 1807 as blue, single-breasted, with flat metal buttons, but becoming grey in 1812, 'corresponding in colour with that established for the men'.

Apparently officers retained the long-tailed coat for dress occasions (Mercer states that at one period Foot Artillery officers had five different jackets); but in January 1812 a short-tailed jacket like that of the rank and file was ordered, but double-breasted, with 'lapels to button over the breast and body'. Slight variations existed, for example in the shape of the gold lace loop (some point-ended, some square). The collar and cuffs were scarlet, the latter with four buttons and loops and the former with one (though one recorded example has no lace on the collar); the lapels could be worn folded back as a scarlet plastron, as well as in the more usual way, with the facing-colour hidden save for turned-back triangles at the neck. The plastron tapered toward the waist, and bore eight or ten horizontal loops, and sometimes one diagonal loop at the top of each lapel. The pockets bore four gold loops and probably sometimes gold edging, and an order of 12 August 1812 notes that a 'triangular ornament' was to be worn on the rear, a lace triangle between the two buttons at waist level on the skirts, similar to the yellow lace decoration on the jackets of the other ranks. Epaulettes with scale straps are also noted at this period. For other ranks there is some evidence that the turnbacks of at least some battalions were scarlet instead of white, though this is unclear.

The 1812 'Belgic' shako was apparently slow in introduction, as only on 3 August 1813 did a Corps General Order state that 'the cap of sugar-loaf shape' be discontinued. The 1812 pattern was like that of the infantry, with white plume and yellow cords for the rank and file, gold and crimson cords for officers. The brass plate was of the standard crowned rococo shield design, with a wide raised border, bearing a reversed 'GR' within a strap inscribed 'ROYAL REGT. OF ARTILLERY', with a mortar flanked by two flaming bombs below. Another variety bears a shield with the Ordnance arms, but whether this was an officers' pattern, a

Sir Augustus Frazer, Royal Horse Artillery: engraving from a portrait post-dating 1815 but depicting the braided dolman and pelisse, which in this case is worn as a cape over both shoulders, with black braid and toggle buttons and gold cords.

musicians', or simply a variety, is not clear. On campaign the shako had a black waterproof cover, with a tube of similar material over the plume. Forage caps worn throughout the period were of varied style, apparently often designed according to the taste of the company commander; Mercer mentions black leather caps (similar to that in Plate C3, without a peak) bearing a 'brass ornament (GR and crown etc.), the leather not stiff, full of cracks and looking rusty, for they were never cleaned'; other sources show a grenade on the front, and latterly the cap was probably of the 'pork pie' style with a larger, flat blue cloth top and red headband.

Musicians' uniforms are unclear; possibly drummers wore 'reversed colours' (i.e. red coats faced blue) but there is no positive evidence. In 1788 drummers had fur caps, but by 1792 'were to have hats the same as those for the Privates and buff belts and slings ... not to have caps, or plain hats, nor laced belts, and slings as heretofore', and it appears

2nd Capt. Richard Bogue, Royal Horse Artillery: print after a portrait by J. Slater, 1812. Note the cravat tied in a bow; the unusual curving arrangement of the braid on the breast of the dolman; and the toggle-buttons of the pelisse set longitudinally along the lines of braid. Bogue was killed at Leipzig in command of the Rocket Troop which served with the Allied armies.

that the uniforms had much decoration removed at this time. In 1788 drummers' coats are noted as having increased in price from 38s. 8d to 52s. 3d, partly as a result of 'a great alteration in the new pattern particularly in the worsted lace with the Ordnance Arms', which presumably was woven lace laid on the seams of the coat and drum carriage ('laced belts') as shown in Dayes' illustrations of the Foot Guards drummers of this date for example; yet by 1792 the price of drummers' coats had fallen to 22s. 1d. George McKenzie noted that when he joined the band in 1795 drummers wore 'Grenadier fur hats', but these may have been restricted to those drummers who played with the band rather than company drummers.

The regimental band wore reversed colours in 1772 (red with blue facings and 'two cheap epaulettes of blue cloth'), plain hats plus one with sergeants' lace with 'Gold Twist loop' for 'First Musician'. In 1785 'Plain Suits' are mentioned; white gaiters in 1788; and shoulder-belts in 1789. For full dress, decorated uniforms were worn, of unknown design; McKenzie noted that in 1795 the band wore 'the three corner cocked hat with a red feather plume'. In 1802 the Master-General of Ordnance altered the uniform, perhaps introducing the white jacket which musician James Lawson thought began c.1805, which had blue facings and a hooked front covered in ½-in. yellow silk lace, with small tassels of red, yellow and blue pendant from the centre of each bow. The blue turnbacks and skirts were edged with ½-in. yellow lace piped scarlet, the pocket flaps blue with three buttons and yellow silk 'frogged ornaments'. The blue collar was edged all round with yellow lace, and bore a button and frogged ornament on each side; the blue cuffs were edged yellow and bore three such ornaments. The epaulettes were yellow silk on blue cloth, the fringe of fine wire covered with spun yellow silk. The uniform was completed by white breeches and black gaiters; a light épeé carried on a black leather waist belt worn under the jacket; and a 'stovepipe' shako with scarlet feather and a brass plate bearing the Ordnance arms. The bandmaster wore a similar uniform, but with gold lace instead of yellow silk, a coat instead of a jacket, a cocked hat with scarlet plume, and gold-tasselled Hessian boots.

At some date before 1812 the popular fashion was followed and the band's percussion section was staffed by Negroes wearing oriental costume. A clothing bill for 1812–13 reveals that the band numbered the bandmaster, one sergeant, two corporals, three 'Blacks' and 31 musicians (including drummers doing duty with the band, and 'Singing boys'!) The bandmaster continued to wear a coat instead of the jacket like the rest, a hat and boots, and gold epaulettes; the 'Blacks' at this time presumably were dressed differently from the remainder as they are listed separately. Normal strength of the band was a master and 18 musicians increased to 20 in October 1802, with two corporals added in 1806 and a sergeant in 1810.

Royal Horse Artillery Uniforms

The Royal Horse Artillery wore a light cavalry style uniform from its inception. The design worn by officers varied with the taste of the individual; always in the regimental dark blue with scarlet facings and gold lace, Mercer describes the initial jacket as based on that of the light dragoons, 'Hooked at the collar, it sloped away towards the little skirt which terminated it behind, and had half facings. On the shoulders a sort of wing made of interwoven rings'—i.e. akin to the 1784 light dragoon coat, with small turnbacks.

In about 1799 this was replaced by a tailless dolman in the current light dragoon style, tight-fitting and single-breasted with three rows of buttons and gold loops on the breast. Mercer notes that in 1804 it was to have 'equal blue and lace . . .

too poor to satisfy us; and as regulations in those days were little adhered to away from headquarters, everyone put on as much more lace as his fancy dictated or his purse permitted . . . my first jacket resembled a furze-bush in full blossom, for it was one mass of gold from the collar to the sash . . . waists were then worn so exceedingly short that my sash was nearly under my arms; and other jackets I had afterwards, of more modest description, had only six

Gunner, Royal Horse Artillery: aquatint by I. C. Stadler after C. Hamilton Smith, from the latter's *Costume of the Army of the British Empire*, published 1 February 1815. This includes the full dress white breeches and Hessian boots, and the sabre suspended from a shoulder belt which has a large brass plate. The cuff-lace is plain, without the trefoil at the point.

loops of lace on the breast. It was the fashion of the day for boys to imitate or try to resemble women, wearing as they did such short waists, and filling out the jacket with handkerchiefs to resemble the female figure'.

The dolman had $\frac{3}{16}$ in. flat gold lace down the front, around the bottom edge and ending at the rear centre in a trefoil knot. An extant example has 24 loops on the breast; two lines of lace were around the $3\frac{1}{2}$-in. collar, the inner line with 'figuring'; the scarlet pointed cuffs had two rows of lace edging, the lower 'figured' and the upper ending in a trefoil at the point, with another trefoil at the rear cuff-seam. The back seams were laced, the upper end with a trefoil at each end. In 1806 this flat lace was replaced by gold cord, and according to Mercer in about 1808 the jacket was given (briefly) a short skirt reaching below the hips. In 1813 it was ordered that 'Officers of RHA to wear the triangular ornament on the embroidered jacket, similar to that worn by the men', i.e. at the rear, as on the Foot Artillery jacket. Buttons probably bore the same design as those of the Foot Artillery, but from c.1811 were of ball pattern, bearing 'GR' within a crowned strap inscribed 'Royal Horse Artillery', 'Royal Horse Artil' or 'Royal Horse Arty'. The other ranks' jacket was similar, but with yellow lace and simpler ornaments (staff sergeants and perhaps sergeants had gold lace), and recorded varieties include cuffs either edged with plain lace or with a trefoil knot.

The horse artillery helmet was the light dragoon 'Tarleton' with black fur crest, leather skull and peak, brass fittings, and a white plume at the left. Mercer thought that the early helmets probably had a leopardskin turban, later changed to crimson silk, and then to blue silk. Efforts were made c.1800 to have this altered, as blue turbans were worn by the despised Corps of Drivers; and in about 1805 black velvet was substituted, changed about a year later to black silk. Mercer noted that 'the form of the helmet formerly was very ugly, straight line at bottom, with the shade or peak sticking straight out, and very large. The bearskin low and poor. By degrees all this was changed ... it became really an elegant article of dress ... an alteration of the base line from straight to curved, which, with the shade, made it droop over the face in front, and into the neck behind ... improving its appearance and its qualities as a defence for the knowledge-box. At the same time the bearskins were raised and made fuller'. The peak-label bore 'Royal Horse Artillery', and at the right side was a badge of 'GR' within a strap bearing the title, though other varieties are recorded including one with three guns, conceivably belonging to the Corps of Drivers, or a volunteer unit. Mercer noted that a chin-chain was an early addition, and that plumes differed with rank as in the Foot Artillery; on service the plume could be encased in a waterpoof cover. The Prince Regent's wardrobe accounts note a black-over-red plume, conceivably for undress (when the bicorn remained popular, as it did in the Foot Artillery). Helmets of the other ranks were similar, of poorer quality manufacture.

Initially leather breeches were worn by all ranks, clothing accounts of 1794 mentioning them and boots with separate spur-leathers. As late as 1799, Mercer notes, pipeclayed buckskins were universal, though dark blue pantaloons 'began to creep in about 1802': 'we wore the blue cloth pantaloons for common undress parades, and the same with gold lace for full dress, etc. The fronts of these were profusely decorated nearly half way down the thigh'. For marching order blue overalls were worn over the breeches, buttoned on the outer seam, and lined with black leather on the inside leg and with leather 'cuffs' shaped like Hessian boots. These were secured under the foot with curb-chain, but when dismounted the chains were 'suspended across the back of the leg by one of the buttons near the knee'. With breeches 'long boots' were worn, 'with a stiff top but not cut out behind, which ... only became regimental afterwards' according to Mercer; but about 1806, he thought, Hessians were worn 'decorated with a silk tassel and having a seam down each side', the lace gold by 1812, with blue stocking-net pantaloons and white leather breeches replacing the white fabric which apparently had been worn some little time before. In November 1806 officers were ordered to wear blue overalls until dinner time, in place of blue pantaloons except for parades; the blue pantaloons were to be worn in the afternoon, and white pantaloons for balls, evening parties and dining out. At a later date pepper-and-salt overalls were introduced; the shade of grey altered more than once, and about 1810–1 red stripes were adopted, with the black leather lining being replaced by brown, with a 3- or 4-in.

Trooper, Mounted Rocket Corps: aquatint by I. C. Stadler after Hamilton Smith, from the latter's *Costume of the Army of the British Empire*, published 2 January 1815. Note the unofficial pennon attached to the rocket sticks, the pouch and waist belts, and the yellow-laced shabraque and valise. The brown leather reinforcing around the ankle is especially deep in this illustration, the red stripe running over the leather.

deep cuff around the ankle. Mercer notes a 'purply half-tint' introduced in 1815. Similar legwear was worn by the rank and file.

Officers' stocks were like those of the Foot Artillery, though Mercer notes the dandified practice of wearing 'an immense number' of cravats, 'put on one over the other, so as to form a mass of considerable thickness, into which the chin was buried almost up to the underlip'. In November 1806 officers were ordered to wear a black velvet stock with an inch of shirt-collar showing over it, and in the evening black silk handkerchiefs instead, still with an inch of collar. Mercer states that crimson silk net sashes were worn until 1815, when hussar-style barrelled sashes were substituted, but probably the hussar pattern was

used earlier; sergeants were noted as wearing silk sashes (at 19s. 6d each) as early as April 1795. Shoulder belts appear to have been worn initially, but replaced by waist belts; from about 1806 black leather belts were worn by officers with the light épée carried in the evening. The belts of the rank and file varied between troops, as in December 1815 Mercer notes that his new troop 'gave up our white cross-belts to G troop, in exchange for their waist-belts, exhibiting thus our old worn jackets in all their nakedness'.

The initial forage cap was blue cloth, shaped like a low, peakless shako, edged with red and 'tied behind with red ferreting' (i.e. laced with red cord at the rear); but captains also issued their troops with caps of their own design, Mercer noting how one captain went to great pains to issue his men with especially ornate caps to distinguish them from the attached Corps of Drivers personnel, only to discover to his great annoyance that the Drivers'

Trooper, Mounted Rocket Corps: print from Congreve's *Details of the Rocket System* (1814). Note the pistol holster on the waist belt, the sabre suspended from the saddle, and the shabraque (bearing 'GPR' below the Prince of Wales' feathers) covering the large rocket-holsters at the front of the saddle.

officer had equipped his men with the same caps on the same day!

Items which increased the 'hussar' appearance of RHA officers were pelisses and sabretaches. The pelisse, Mercer thought, was first introduced *c.* 1805, 'poor shabby concerns . . . trimmed with some brown fur . . . the braiding on the breast also was sparse and of very small cord . . . Somewhere about 1808 the pelisse, only tolerated before, became a regular and authorized part of our uniform. The sable fur gave place to the grey astrachan, the braiding became richer with barrel buttons, and the whole affair more Hussarish'. Portraits show different patterns, black braid and 'toggle' buttons appearing popular. Mentions of the pelisse are probably confused by the same term being in contemporary use for a braided frock coat worn in undress, a General Order of 14 January 1812 describing for ordinary duty 'a short surtout, which is calculated to be worn likewise as a pelisse on service'.

Sabretaches were apparently unregulated, Thomas Dyneley ordering one in August 1812 'with ink-stand, lock and key, etc., and two knots'; though two paintings in the Royal Collection dating from *c.*1810 show pure hussar uniform, the officer with a grey-furred pelisse and both officer and gunner with a crimson sash with gold and yellow barrels respectively. The officer has a red pouch-belt ornamented with gilt studs, and a red sabretache with gold lace edge, bearing a gold crown over three guns over three cannon balls. The gunner's sabretache is black, bearing a brass crown over a flaming grenade, over two more grenades. Both wear scarlet mirliton caps with black wing edged gold, and gold cords (yellow for the gunner). Both have point-ended dark blue shabraques edged gold (or yellow), the officer's with a crowned 'GR' over a laurel spray in both front and rear corners, and the gunner a crown over letters 'RHA' in script in the same positions. If accurate, they probably represent a temporary full dress perhaps restricted to a single troop.

The Royal Horse Artillery was armed with sabres (of the 1796 light dragoon pattern from that date) and pistols; the first issue was apparently a batch of 80 double-barrelled flintlocks ordered from Henry Nock at £8 each, with side-by-side 18-in. barrels, of which one was rifled, with browned barrels and a

Ammunition-horse, Mounted Rocket Corps: print from Congreve's *Details of the Rocket System* (1814). The cover of the rocket panniers bears the same badge as shown on the shabraque of the rocket-troopers.

'shifting butt', i.e. a detachable stock (supplied by Nock at 10s. each) to turn the gun into a carbine. Its great weight (7 lb 12 oz) made it virtually impossible to use with one hand. Mercer notes that officers carried a regulation sabre and smaller undress sword, 'usually so crooked as to be useless as anything but a reaping hook. The regulation itself, though an excellent sword for cutting, was bad for using the point . . . Dandyism with the sword was to wear it trailing along the ground', with 'a little treek or wheel in the end of the scabbard'.

The hussar appearance of the RHA was especially evident in 1815 Mercer noting that before Waterloo Norman Ramsey ('H' Troop) wore a light cavalry belt instead of a sash, Robert Bull ('I' Troop) and others beards and moustaches, and Mercer himself ('G' Troop) a moustache, which with his pelisse ('plain and rather shabby') made him resemble a Prussian hussar, he thought! Mercer appropriated a French lance at Waterloo, which was carried thereafter by his groom/orderly, and was later used as the prototype for the lance introduced as a weapon into the British cavalry.

Mounted Rocket Corps Uniforms

The senior Rocket Troop, Capt. Bogue's, became the 2nd Troop in 1813, and fought at Leipzig, where Bogue was killed; the junior Troop, Capt. Eliot's, was numbered the 1st, fought in the

Artillery on the march: print after John A. Atkinson from his *Picturesque Representation of the ... Costumes of Great Britain*, published by Miller and Walker, 1 January 1807. The central figure is an officer of the RHA, wearing a 'Tarleton' helmet; the other mounted officer is from the Foot Artillery, in bicorn. At the left are two members of the Corps of Drivers, one with (apparently) a peaked cap bearing 'CD/RA', but the one in profile evidently without a peak.

Peninsula and, under Capt. Whinyates, at Waterloo. Being affiliated to the RHA they wore horse artillery uniform, plus a pouch belt over the left shoulder, a pistol holster at the left hip, butt forward, and perhaps the sabre attached to the saddle; contrary to some modern reconstructions it would seem highly unlikely that the double-barrelled RHA pistol was still in use.

Attached to the saddle by means of a carbine-style bucket was a bundle of three or four rocket sticks, which for a time had a white-over-light-blue pennon affixed—quite unofficially and discontinued by the time of Waterloo according to Whinyates. The shabraque was blue, point-ended with yellow lace edging and ornaments; Hamilton Smith shows a badge of a crown over 'GPR' in front and rear corners ('George, Prince Regent'); Congreve's *Details of the Rocket System* (London 1814) shows a badge at the front of the shabraque only, of the Prince of Wales' feathers over 'GPR'. Hamilton Smith shows a circular blue valise with yellow edge, bearing 'A' over 'RR' over 'C', presumably representing 'Royal Artillery Rocket Corps'. The rockets were carried in the saddle holsters, with a spear head to turn a seven-foot rocket-stick into a lance if necessary.

Corps of Drivers Uniforms

The early artillery drivers (civilians hired under contract) appear to have worn white or grey frock coats with blue collar and cuffs and black jockey caps or cocked hats; these are shown in pictures from the 1770s, and a battery inspection of 1798 records drivers wearing white smocks with blue collar and cuffs. A print of the mid-1790s shows the uniform as in Plate A4, a plain (civilian) agricultural smock with an artillery hat and gaiters. Clothing accounts in July 1793 mention 'frocks' and leather caps; in April 1794 coat, waistcoat and leggings (together costing £1 15s. 4d), hat, stable dress frock, 'trowsers' and 'foraging cap', and brown cloth gaiters. In May 1794 'jackets' and 'shagg breeches' are mentioned (approximately one-third cheaper than those used before), and a further re-designing must have occurred in June 1796, as a Board of Ordnance Minute notes that 'the trowsers in store at the Tower for Drivers could be altered to the present pattern at 2s. 8d each, that the brown cloth gaiters would serve for the French Artillery, and that the coats might be converted to the use of the marching battalions by altering the linings and facings which would cost 7s. 2d each coat'. By December 1795 the 'Tarleton' helmet had been adopted by some drivers, according to a

Minute regarding the payment for '100 helmet caps supplied for Captain Commissary Churchill's Drivers', though in July 1795 600 caps are mentioned, for which the manufacturer Hawkes was paid 2s. each. An extant oval brass badge is perhaps that worn on the helmet at this time: it bears a shield with Ordnance arms and the inscription 'GUNNER DRIVERS' below.

By c.1806 the uniform of the Corps of Drivers was that shown in Plate C3. The 'Tarleton' was later re-adopted (or worn concurrently with the black leather cap?), with a blue turban. Two styles of jacket are depicted later, one exactly like that of the Foot Artillery with bastion loops, but with a collar loop and plain red shoulder straps edged yellow. The other style is similarly coloured, but with pointed cuffs and three rows of buttons on the breast, with a 'frame' of lace around the lines of buttons; these two styles are depicted in Plates G3 and G4. It is unclear when these uniforms were used; it is sometimes stated that the Foot Artillery jacket was worn prior to the adoption of the one with three rows of buttons, but it is equally possible that the different companies wore different uniform. Conceivably the Foot Artillery drivers wore the Foot Artillery jacket and those attached to the RHA, the one with three rows of buttons. Hamilton Smith's plate (published 1 June 1815) shows the forage cap of the 'pork pie' shape with flat blue cloth top and red head band. Sauerweid in late 1815 or

Artillery, c.1800: a team (evidently of the Foot Artillery), with a driver running alongside the leading horse, wearing a leather cap and frock-coat, probably white with blue collar and cuffs. (Print after W. H. Pyne)

early 1816 shows a driver wearing an extremely voluminous grey greatcoat with deep cuffs and an elbow-length cape with standing collar.

* * *

'Battalion Guns'

Supplementing the ordinary artillery were light fieldpieces attached to infantry battalions, intended to provide immediate fire-support for the unit. Infantry battalions trained an officer and 34 men to handle the unit's two 6-pdr. guns, and cavalry regiments had an officer and 18 men to crew their mobile 'galloper guns'. The system was not a success and had become virtually extinct by 1799. Generally, the guns were found to be more of an encumbrance than an asset; as the French general Lespinasse wrote in 1800, 'If you want to prevent your troops manoeuvring, embarrass them with guns'. Until 1798 artillery personnel were supplied to train and supervise the 'battalion gunners'.

Foreign Artillery

Prior to 1803 a number of *émigré* units existed, formed originally of French royalists, most notably Rotalier's and de Quiefdeville's French corps and Nacquard's Dutch. Rotalier's were largely French

Driver, Royal Artillery: print after Carle Vernet, c.1815–16. The uniform shown is obviously that resembling the Foot Artillery jacket: the bastion-shaped breast-loops are especially clear. The sheepskin is white with red wolf-teeth edging, worn over a light grey blanket with red and blue stripes near the edge.

and the volunteers, the latter restricted almost exclusively to manning shore batteries, as with few exceptions field-pieces were not entrusted to them: as the Duke of Richmond wrote in 1794, 'it would be improper to trust movable Artillery to Volunteer Corps on the Coast where they would be liable to be taken by the Enemy'. In December 1803 there were 102 volunteer companies, totalling 8,917 men, most of which were very competent, though in some cases the standard was erratic. When the Sunderland company practised shooting at a derelict boat, some old sailors watching remarked that the safest place for onlookers was to 'gan an' sit i' the boat'; while the Cromer Sea Fencibles (corps also trained to man shore-batteries) in 1804 accidentally shot off the foot of their own captain and the leg of a surgeon! Among inland units which did possess mobile guns were the Honourable Artillery Company (London), the Bradford Volunteers, and the single horse unit, the Bedfordshire Horse Artillery.

Engineers

The Corps of Royal Engineers was composed exclusively of officers and though highly trained, was tiny: in 1792 there were but 73, and by 1813 the number had risen only to 262. Under the Ordnance and trained at Woolwich, the engineers occupied a unique position in that they were the only officers whose pay increased when serving abroad, and they tended to be consulted only on special occasions such as the undertaking of a major siege, bridge building or surveying—tasks not easily accomplished by officers of other branches. Many senior officers were old and inactive (like the Board of Ordnance, 'all ... inherent pomp and acquired gravity' according to Blakeney), so that much of the work was thrown upon a small number of junior ranks, whose casualties were horrific: 102 engineer officers served in the Peninsular War, 25 of whom died (24 in action and one from exhaustion). Even in the most exposed positions, their experience at San Sebastian was typical: 11 out of 18 became casualties. So severe were the losses that Wellington remarked, 'We have had such an expenditure of engineers that I can hardly wish for any body, les

naval gunners, almost wiped out at Quiberon; de Quiefdeville's never reached more than cadre strength, and its commander transferred to Portuguese service; Naquard's served in the West Indies. All wore blue uniforms with red facings, and were consolidated into the Royal Foreign Artillery (disbanded 1817), which served in the West Indies under Nacquard; their uniform was like that of the Royal Artillery but for the wording on the accoutrements.

Volunteer Artillery
Unlike the infantry, which eventually was allowed to recruit ready-trained men from the Militia, the artillery had no such reservoir of trained personnel—an important consideration when assessing the problem of manpower. Second-line artillery comprised the static garrison companies

the same fate befall him as has befallen so many'. To supplement these meagre resources, line officers were appointed as assistant-engineers, many of whom were unskilled. (Though not all: for example, Capt. Blakiston of the 17th Portuguese Regt. who served as a volunteer engineer at San Sebastian had trained with the Madras Engineers, and was responsible for blowing in the gate at Vellore during the mutiny there.)

Though the Royal Engineers were skilled and well led (in the Peninsula by the celebrated Richard Fletcher until his death at San Sebastian) and achieved prodigies (most notably the Lines of Torres Vedras), until late in the period their support was almost nil. The rank and file of the engineer service were provided by the Royal Military Artificers and Labourers (Royal Military Artificers from 1798), 12 companies of 'tradesmen', each commanded by a sub-lieutenant (always a retired NCO) plus a staff sergeant seconded from the Royal Artillery. These troops performed the building and carpentry in fortresses, eight companies being stationed in Britain, two in Gibraltar, one in the West Indies and one in Nova Scotia, where

they remained from the end of the American War until 1811, 'in what may ... be styled a state of vegetation ... a vast number of men, who had actually grown grey in the Corps, who had never entered a transport, nor made a single day's march'.

For campaigns, small detachments were sent from these companies, whose commanders kept their best men and sent to the field army 'the stupidest and least trustworthy non-commissioned officers, and ... the most ignorant profligate and abandoned of the privates'. 'A set of undisciplined vagabonds' was how one engineer officer described the Artificers, and so low was the corps rated that in the Mediterranean units of Maltese and Sicilian pioneers were found more effective. Only small detachments were sent to the Peninsula: total strength in November 1809 was two sergeants and 23 other ranks, of whom four were ill and two missing; they were reinforced by 25 men who had

Corps of Drivers, Royal Artillery: aquatint by I. C. Stadler after C. Hamilton Smith, from the latter's *Costume of the Army of the British Empire*, published 1 June 1815. The driver (right) wears the jacket with three rows of buttons, and corporal's chevrons; upon the waggon is a man in undress, with the flat cloth forage cap.

never 'seen a sap, battery or trench constructed'. At Ciudad Rodrigo only 18 artificers could be mustered, and eight at Burgos, manual labour being performed by unskilled infantrymen.

After the carnage of Badajoz Wellington demanded that trained artificers be provided ('It is inconceivable with what disadvantage we undertake any thing like a siege for want of assistance of this description'); and in April 1812 the 'Royal Military Artificers or Sappers and Miners' were formed (Royal Sappers and Miners from 1813), consisting of 2,800 rank and file with Royal Engineer officers to command companies, the men no longer serving in *ad hoc* detachments. Trained at Chatham, there were 300 present with the Peninsular army for the 1813 campaign, and from San Sebastian onwards they made a significant contribution; at Bergen-op-Zoom they actually led the assault and were the the first upon the enemy ramparts. In 1815 each Division had an engineer 'brigade' attached, each brigade comprising a Sapper and Miner company with their own tools, and waggon-transport to convey enough entrenching tools for 500 infantrymen. Prior to this the engineer services (and even the pontoon train) had *no* transport, being dependent upon whatever the artillery could spare. In 1815 the field army had 41 engineer officers, 800 Sappers and Miners, and 550 drivers with 160 engineer waggons and over 1,000 horses; only the drivers were an imperfect body, recruited partly from the RA Drivers and partly from hired Belgians, 'ignorant of their duty and many of them of bad character'.

Royal Engineers' Uniforms

As employees of the Board of Ordnance, the Royal Engineers from 1782 wore blue coats faced with black velvet, with gold epaulette, white lining, waistcoat and breeches, and crimson sash. The head-dress was a bicorn, with the 'round hat' sanctioned for hot climates, and a crested hat like that of the Royal Artillery is shown worn by Col. Moncrieff, the Chief Engineer, in De Loutherberg's picture of Valenciennes. A description of the coat for 1798 notes superfine blue cloth with black Genoa velvet lapels, cuffs and standing collar, nine twist button holes in the lapels, three-pointed pocket flaps with four button holes, four buttons per cuff with cloth-covered buttons opening the rear of

the cuff, white turnbacks with a button as ornament, two buttons at the rear and 'lapells short of the waist'.

The blue uniform was easily confused; as Rice Jones wrote in 1809, 'From our uniform being like the French we were sometimes mistaken for officers of that nation', and from 1811 a new uniform was introduced; as Major William Nicholas wrote, 'Our uniform is changed to scarlet with a gold-laced dress-coat. I dislike the change on account of the colour and the expence; but I shall order nothing till I know whether I am to have the brevet rank; as it makes a difference in the epaulettes'. The new uniform was still in infantry style, but in scarlet with 'Garter blue' facings (a lighter shade than the ordinary dark blue facings of 'royal' regiments). The lapels are depicted with turned-back 'triangles' or fastened over, and extant examples and portraits have sewn-back blue plastron lapels, narrowing slightly towards the waist, with 11 point-ended loops on each lapel, one on each side of the collar, four on the cuffs and pockets, and four loops by the two buttons at the rear waist. Epaulettes were gold, with gold knots on dark blue figure-of-eight patches on the turnbacks. An extant white waistcoat has white hussar braid in 23 rows, with three rows of cloth-covered buttons on the breast, and breeches with white Austrian knots on the thighs; as shown by Hamilton Smith, overalls were the usual wear on active service. The buttons bore the royal cypher within a crowned strap inscribed 'ROYAL ENGINEERS'.

Royal Military Artificers' Uniforms

Information on the Artificers' uniform is contained in the unit history, published 1855/57, whose author T. W. J. Connolly, is believed to have had access to material no longer extant. From 1787 the uniform comprised a blue infantry-style coat with black facings and falling collar, square-ended loops, white turnbacks, white waistcoat and breeches, black gaiters, and bicorn bound with yellow lace, with yellow loop, black cockade and red tuft. Infantry equipment for sergeants included a spontoon and a straight-bladed sword with iron knuckle-bow, which they purchased personally; drummers had short swords with brass mounts. Rank-distinctions were: labourers, yellow lace on hat and coat; artificers, finer cloth, gold lace on hat

1: Field officer, Royal Artillery; 1793-94
2: Gunner, Royal Artillery, c.1793
3: Corporal, Royal Artillery, c.1795
4: Driver, Royal Artillery, c.1795

A

1: Battalion gunner, Bucks. Militia, c.1794
2: Artificer, RMA&L, c.1795
3: Artificer, working dress, c.1795
4: Officer, Royal Artillery, c. 1797

B

1: Corporal, Royal Artillery, c.1806
2: Gunner, Royal Artillery, c.1809
3: Driver, Royal Artillery, c.1806
4: 3rd Class Pte., Royal Staff Corps, c.1810

C

1: Officer, Royal Engineers, c.1810
2: Private, Royal Military Artificers, c.1809
3: Officer, Royal Waggon Train, c.1812
4: Commissary

D

1: Field officer, Royal Artillery, 1814
2: Company Sgt., Royal Artillery, 1814
3: Gunner, Royal Artillery, 1814

E

1: Officer, Royal Engineers, 1813
2: Corporal, Royal Sappers & Miners, 1813
3: Sgt., RS&M, working dress, 1813
4: Pte., RS&M, trench dress, 1813

F

1: Tpr., Mounted Rocket Corps, RHA, 1814
2: Corporal, Royal Horse Artillery, 1815
2: Driver, Corps of Drivers, RA, 1815
4: Farrier, Corps of Drivers, RA, 1815

G

1: Quartermaster, RHA, 1815
2: Officer, RHA, 1815
3: Assistant surgeon, infantry, c. 1815

drummers, as artificers, but broad lace bearing the Ordnance arms; corporals, as artificer, with yellow shoulder knots (on both shoulders in some companies, on the right shoulder in others, including the Woolwich company), with yellow fringes authorised but privately-purchased gold fringes permitted; sergeants, gold-laced hat, laced shoulder straps without fringe, crimson sash; sergeant majors, as sergeant but gold lace on coat, bullion epaulettes.

In working dress all except sergeant majors wore a plain canvas or 'ravenduck' frock, almost to the ankles, single-breasted with three brass buttons and turndown collar, plain black felt 'round hat', white duck waistcoat and 'gaiter-trousers', and queued but unpowdered hair. Corporals and sergeants had an inch-wide gold band around the base of the hat, and whiter-coloured frocks. Although the 'Soldier Artificer Company' at Gibraltar was not fully integrated into the corps until 1797, they wore the corps' uniform from 1789.

In 1792 the bicorn was replaced by a 'round hat', upright collars were introduced, and drummers' lace changed from the Ordnance arms to a mixture of black, red and yellow, with wings added to the coat. The long working-frock was replaced by a plain white duck jacket, or in winter a blue jacket with black collar and cuffs. In 1794 the hats became white, but black again in 1795, with rosette and crimson plume for sergeants, and their previous gold hat-band. Skirts were added to the working jacket in 1795, with pockets, a yellow triangle between the two rear skirt-buttons, and a yellow loop on the collar (gold for sergeants). In 1797 the bicorn was re-introduced, with black binding, yellow or gold cockade loop and an 8-in. white plume; sergeants and sergeant majors had gold silk lace woven in a flower pattern. At the corners of the hat were gold rosettes, worn by all except labourers. The coat became single-breasted, with shorter skirts; lapels were replaced by bastion breast loops. Drummers wore red jackets, with the previous lace; queues continued to be worn but were henceforth unpowdered at all times.

In 1801 working dress consisted of a blue cloth jacket, sleeved serge waistcoat, black round hat, blue serge pantaloons and black short gaiters; those who had served in Egypt were permitted to wear a sphinx on their appointments. From the outset, the white leather belts had brass buckles, not belt plates. The shako was adopted in 1802, with white plume and a plate which apparently bore a shield with Ordnance arms (see Plate D2).

Royal Sappers & Miners' Uniforms

The Sappers and Miners' uniform was in the 1812 infantry style: red jacket with blue facings and yellow bastion loops, white breeches and black gaiters for dress, and grey overalls for service wear. NCOs' chevrons were yellow, and sergeants' sashes were crimson with a central dark blue stripe. The headdress was the 'Belgic' shako, with white plume and yellow cords; and though the Connolly prints show large plates, Hamilton Smith appears to depict a plate of ordinary shape—conceivably Connolly's artist portrayed a 'stovepipe' shako-plate on the wrong pattern of cap. Buttons were like those of the Engineers but with the appropriate title. The working dress of the corps is described under Plates F3 and F4.

* * *

Foreign Engineers

A corps of Maltese artificers was formed to accompany the expedition to Egypt in 1800–01, who wore Ordnance uniform. Two companies of Maltese Artificers were raised in January 1806, later three, for Mediterranean service, officered by the Royal Engineers. They wore blue jackets with black collar and cuffs, Ordnance buttons, blue cloth pantaloons and 'military hat and feather'; perhaps with yellow loops like the British artificers. In 1808 they were clothed in cotton uniforms, with black facings; sergeants had sashes and the sergeant major wore British artificer uniform. They were absorbed by the Sappers and Miners in 1813. Other 'foreign' engineer corps included a number of French émigré officers, ex-members of the French engineers, who served in Holland, Quiberon, the West Indies and Portugal; they may have retained French uniform or adopted that of the Royal Engineers, though two who received temporary commissions in the Royal Engineers were ordered at the Cape to wear the same uniform as in Europe, red faced yellow.

Royal Staff Corps

The Royal Staff Corps was authorised in 1798 to provide an engineer service under the control of the

Horse Guards rather than the Master-General of Ordnance; initially a headquarters and four companies, it was increased to battalion size in 1809, its companies being employed piecemeal and officers on detached duty. Trained and equipped as infantry, the Staff Corps was responsible for field defences and fortification; officers were employed on a variety of tasks, overlapping those of the Royal Engineers and the Quartermaster-General's department, as guides and surveyors as well as engineers: for example, the repair of the bridge at Alcantara in 1812, and the bridge of boats over the Adour (1813) were the work of Col. Sturgeon of the Staff Corps. Their intended rôle as overseers of less-skilled men is demonstrated by the gradation of ranks. Each company had a sergeant major and quartermaster sergeant, and the rank of 'sergeant-overseer' also existed; the privates were divided into 1st, 2nd, and 3rd classes, the 1st class intended to act as sergeants in charge of unskilled labourers, the 2nd class as corporals and the 3rd class as lance corporals—even the 3rd class privates received more pay than an infantryman.

The Staff Corps uniform was of infantry style, scarlet with dark blue facings, without lace loops; dark blue pantaloons were worn with short gaiters

A 'battalion gun' in the field: print by W. H. Pyne, published 1802. The gun is advancing by *bricole* (manhandled by drag-ropes) by infantrymen who appear to wear light company caps; most wear one-piece 'gaiter-trousers'. At the extreme left is a man in a fur-crested 'round hat', probably a member of the Royal Artillery acting as an instructor.

or half boots. In 1801 the Inspection Return notes that their muskets were smaller than those in general use, unable to take ordinary ball ammunition, i.e. of smaller calibre. Sergeants are noted as carrying swords and shoulder belts and wearing sashes, and the corps included four buglers with horns. Hamilton Smith's plate of 1813 shows the 'Belgic' cap with white-over-red plume but no cords, a jacket still devoid of lace, and with a badge on the left upper arm bearing '1' or '2' for 1st and 2nd class privates, and blue pantaloons with short gaiters. By this date the shoulder belts had given way to a belt over the left shoulder for the cartridge box, and a white leather waist belt with rectangular buckle supporting the bayonet scabbard; the firearm appears to be a short musketoon. The 1812 clothing instructions note grey pantaloons, half boots, and a 'round jacket' and grey wool 'open trousers', probably as a working dress. Officers probably wore infantry-style uniform, but with cuffs and sleeve buttons in staff style, i.e. with the buttons set vertically up the sleeve, with dummy loops of twist embroidery. Their shoulder belt plate appears to have been a gilt oval with silver beaded rim, bearing a 16-point silver star with a blue centre bearing a red-enamelled silver coronet, encircled by a gilt crowned strap inscribed 'British Staff'. The Cavalry Staff Corps (formed 1813) is covered in *Wellington's Light Cavalry* (B. Fosten, MAA 126, London 1982).

Commissariat & Transport

The army's commissariat was run by the Treasury and commissaries were thus civilians outside military discipline, which in part explains the failings of the system. Totally untrained for active service and beset by countless clerical regulations, it is not surprising that many commissariat officers were inefficient, or that many were dismissed for peculation, given that their home-service pay of 15 s. per diem dropped to 5 s. on campaign! Many were appointed through patronage by Treasury officials, leading to countless complaints; Wellington wrote that his commissariat 'is very incompetent ... the people who manage it are incapable of managing anything outside a counting house'.

Only in 1810 were any qualifications required; after that date all commissaries had to be 16 years of age at least, with a year's clerking experience, but not until 1812 was an examination in English and arithmetic instituted. One of the first candidates was found to have been cashiered from the army, and another (appointed by patronage of the Navy Treasurer) wrote that he was 'lernging a letel French'! In the Talavera campaign Sir William Payne Bt. addressed the assembled cavalry commissaries: 'Owing to the exertions it would entail, a commissary who did his duty in this country could not possibly remain alive. He would be forced to die. Of all my commissaries, not one has yet sacrificed his life; consequently they are not doing their duty'—to which the German commissary Schaumann commented, 'Most Englishmen of high position, particularly when they are serving in a hot climate, are a little mad'!

Assistant-Commissaries, their Deputies and clerks, were attached to each infantry brigade and cavalry regiment; their superiors were the Commissary-General and his Assistants and Deputies, but even these were imperfect: Wellington dismissed one Deputy Commissary-General in 1811 with the words, 'the service would be still further embarrassed if you continued to conduct it'. In 1809 Wellington had to write to Gen. Sherbrooke that whilst he understood the general's fury at 'the neglect and incapacity of some of the Officers of the Commissariat, by which we have suffered and are still suffering so much', in future such incompetents should be reported to headquarters 'rather than they should be abused by the General Officers of the Army'! The story that Picton threatened to hang a commissary may not be very exaggerated.

A military transport service had been tried in 1794, with waggons and horses bought by the

A gun-team resting: print by W. H. Pyne, published 1802. The gunners are apparently members of a battalion gun-team; the officer wears an undress stocking cap, probably of his own design. The driver (right) wears a typical agricultural smock and apparently a leather or cloth undress cap.

Most volunteer artillery wore a uniform based upon that of the Royal Artillery. This gunner of the Honourable Artillery Company has a 'Tarleton' helmet with leopardskin turban, white plume, gilt fittings but silver badge; blue jacket with scarlet collar, cuffs and wings with gold lace, gilt buttons and silver plumes badge on the wing, and no turnbacks; white breeches and black gaiters, with a white belt with oval gilt plate suspending a curved sabre in a black leather scabbard with gilt chape. He is in the act of ramming home a charge. (Print by Hill and Hopwood, after James Green, 1804.)

government; but of the 'Corps of Royal Waggoners' as Commissary-General Havilland LeMesurier wrote, 'little need be said, as its miserable state became proverbial in the Army; it failed completely in every part, and the only trace remaining of it is a heavy charge on the half-pay list'. Thereafter, the Treasury refused to establish a military transport service, relying instead upon hired local civilians, which in the Peninsular War meant Portuguese muleteers and ponderous ox-carts. As a result the inefficiencies of the commissariat multiplied; as Wellington wrote in January 1812, 'What do you think of empty cars taking two days to go ten miles on a good road ... I am obliged to appear satisfied

or they would all desert'. An extreme case is quoted by Sir Alexander Dickson, a detachment of whose gunners in October 1809 marched 436 miles to collect 20 uniforms!

In August 1799 a Royal Waggon Train was formed for service in Holland, the men mostly drafted from the cavalry with NCOs commissioned as subalterns. Initially of five troops, each of three sergeants, three corporals, one trumpeter, three artificers and 62 privates, it was increased during the Peninsular War by the incorporation of two troops of the Irish Commissariat Corps of Waggoners (already serving in Portugal), and in 1814 numbered 14 troops with 1,903 other ranks. Equipped with their own teams, the Waggon Train could only solve a fraction of the army's transportation problems, and that not with complete success. Schaumann wrote of their commander, Digby Hamilton, in Spain: 'Fat general Hamilton of the wagon train has also turned up here with his useless wagon corps', and the unit's nickname 'Newgate Blues' (from Newgate gaol) is testimony of its reputation!

Royal Waggon Train Uniforms

The Waggon Train initially wore blue uniforms faced red, changing to red faced blue in 1811. No chevrons were worn according to the 1803 Clothing Warrant, by which sergeants were to have silver-laced jackets and corporals silver lace on collar and cuffs. The red uniform is shown by Hamilton Smith in a print dated 1 April 1812, as the light cavalry style of Plate D3, with a bicorn, but a shako of the 1812 light dragoon pattern was also worn, with silver lace band and rosette, and silver chinscale with rose bosses. The other ranks wore red jacket with blue facings and three rows of white buttons in a white lace 'frame' like that of the Artillery Drivers, white lace trimming on the facings, and white-laced light dragoon shako. Other items noted are blue foraging caps, white stable jacket, blue breeches and 'Russian Duck' overalls. They were armed with carbines and bayonets; officers carried light cavalry sabres from a waist belt, but shoulder belts were also used (probably earlier), with an oval gilt plate bearing 'GR' within a crowned strap inscribed 'Royal Waggoners'. A later (?) pattern had the centre in blue enamel and the inscription 'ROYAL WAGGON TRAIN'.

Medical Services

The army's medical service was superintended by the Medical Board, consisting of the Surgeon General, Physician General and the Inspector General of Hospitals, who were civilians with private practices, which contributed towards the evils which afflicted the army medical service. When the Physician General was asked to investigate 'Walcheren fever' he declined with the excuse that 'he was not acquainted with the diseases of soldiers in camp and quarters'. The Board was finally replaced by a Director General, but with little improvement; the Duke of York called him 'an old driveller'.

Standards of medical care were low, the shortage of personnel resulting in the appointment of half-trained surgeons: 'not a few apothecaries and even druggists' apprentices found their way into the service', according to James McGrigor. John Moore's 51st Foot had a classic example of such a surgeon: 'completely ignorant, devoid of humanity, and a rogue ... against his ignorance I have no remedy, tho' I have daily the grossest instances of it'. Medical supplies were the responsibility of the Apothecary General, and non-medical supplies for hospital use that of the Purveyor General (the former a *hereditary* office since 1747 ...); and hospitals were almost invariably insanitary and ill-administered places where the chance of recovery was not good. The situation improved markedly after the appointment of the capable humanitarian Dr. James McGrigor as Inspector General of Hospitals in the Peninsula in late 1811. His establishment of prefabricated, portable hospitals which accompanied the army's march saved thousands from the agonising trip in unsprung carts which they would otherwise have had to endure, there being no properly-designed ambulance waggons whatever.

Each battalion had a surgeon (ranking as a captain) and two assistant surgeons (ranking as lieutenants); there were no trained orderlies or ambulance personnel. Though most regimental surgeons did their best to assuage the appalling injuries caused by Napoleonic warfare, medical knowledge was sufficiently limited that an experienced surgeon could write after Vimeiro: 'a simple

Maj. William Nicholas wearing the uniform of the Royal Engineers: engraving by E. Scriven after a drawing made by Lt. B. Pym at Cadiz, 1812. The coat is shown here fastened across the breast, and totally devoid of lace. Nicholas was mortally wounded at Badajoz in circumstances of the greatest gallantry.

inspection of their wounds, with a few words of consolation, or perhaps a little opium, was all that could be recommended ... prudence equally forbids the rash interposition of unavailing art, and the useless indulgence of delusive hope'.

Associated with the medical service were the **army chaplains**. Though each regiment was supposed initially to have one clergyman, hardly any were present. (In 1796 Rev. Peter Vataas of the 14th Light Dragoons had been on paid leave for 52 years.) The total failure of the system led to the abolition of regimental chaplains, and few were prepared to accompany the army on campaign. A small number of devoted clergymen served in the Peninsula, especially Samuel Briscall, who was attached to Wellington's headquarters, whom the Duke described as 'an excellent young man ... excepting Mr. Denis at Lisbon ... I believe Mr. Briscall is the only chaplain doing his duty'. Despite Wellington's distrust of the non-conformist meetings which increased in the Peninsular army—'I believe a sergeant now and then gives them a

Field Officer, Royal Engineers (right), and private, Royal Sappers and Miners (left): aquatint by I. C. Stadler after Charles Hamilton Smith, from the latter's *Costume of the Army of the British Empire*, published 2 January 1815. The officer has the 1796 infantry sword with metal scabbard and suspended from a waist belt, as field officers were permitted to wear; the lapels are folded partly back to reveal lace loops. The sapper apparently carries the Foot Artillery sword, and has a shako plate like that of the general pattern, not the large plate shown by Connolly. Note that the jacket has no shoulder tufts.

sermon'—and despite the appointment of Briscall as Wellington's domestic chaplain, the clergy received little encouragement: 'Briscall, say as much as you like in five and twenty minutes. I shall not stay longer'.

Medical Services Uniforms

Medical staff officers wore staff-pattern single-breasted scarlet coats faced with black velvet, with lines of 'twist' embroidery on the breast, and indented cuffs with two buttons and embroidered loops on the sleeve, two buttons on the cuff for Medical Inspectors and one for lower ranks. Buttons were gilt and epaulettes gold, two worn by higher ranks and one by Apothecaries and Hospital Mates, the latter having red cuffs with no buttons. Purveyors wore the same distinctions, but with silver epaulettes and buttons, their deputies with a single epaulette. Regimental surgeons wore a combination of regimental and medical style, their coats single-breasted with embroidered loops on the breast, but facings in regimental colouring, with regimental lace, buttons and epaulettes. Their sword was suspended from a narrow black waist belt. Medical staff wore bicorns and regimental surgeons normally the head-dress of their unit, with the black plume restricted to the medical and Judge-Advocate's departments.

The Plates

A1: Field Officer, Royal Artillery, campaign dress, 1793–94
This figure is based on De Loutherberg's picture 'The Siege of Valenciennes' and the portrait of Sir William Congreve prepared for it. The hat is a version of the 'round hat' worn by officers in the Netherlands in 1793–94, with fur crest, large cockade at the left and three gold cords around the crown, as shown in other contemporary sources such as the portrait of an officer named Stehelin. De Loutherberg shows the sash worn beneath the coat

Royal Military Artificers and Labourers, 1795: print after G. B. Campion from Connolly's *History of the Royal Sappers and Miners*. Shown here is the 1795-pattern working jacket with short skirts and yellow lace triangle at the rear, black collar and cuffs with collar loop; the sergeant (right) has a hat plume and lace band, and both wear one-piece 'gaiter-trousers'.

Royal Military Artificers and Labourers, 1794: print after G. B. Campion from Connolly's *History of the Royal Sappers and Miners*. Depicted here is the working dress, with the white hat worn briefly in 1794–95, with the tailless working jacket in blue with black collar and cuffs (left) or white for summer (right). The NCO (centre) wears a black hat with gold band. The 'round hats' appear somewhat Victorian in style; conceivably those actually worn did not widen towards the top so markedly.

in the usual manner, and topped riding boots; horse furniture consists of a white sheepskin saddle cover with black bearskin holster caps.

A2: Gunner, Royal Artillery, c.1793

Based on a watercolour by Edward Dayes, this shows the Royal Artillery uniform at the outbreak of the Revolutionary Wars. The leather equipment changed little in design over the entire period, and was white throughout, including the cartridge box, the flap of which bore a brass crown with a scroll below, inscribed with the name of the Corps and battalion number, the badge mounted on a red cloth patch. No shoulder belt plate was worn, the front of the belt instead having leather 'tubes' to accommodate a small hammer and two pickers (for clearing the vents of cannon). A powder horn with metal nozzle and cap (inscribed with battalion and company identification) was carried upon a scarlet cord on the belt over the left shoulder. Dayes shows the knapsack as grey painted canvas, bearing a blue disc edged red, bearing a yellow crown with red cap over the white letters 'RA' over '--Battn.'

A3: Corporal, Royal Artillery, c.1795

This depicts the Royal Artillery uniform after the introduction of the 'Mother Shipton' round hat, which existed in several versions; the yellow epaulettes were the principal rank distinction. The sabre carried at this period is uncertain, but was probably like the 1751/52 'pattern' (which was not strictly regulated), with triple-bar brass hilt and slightly curved blade.

A4: Driver, Royal Artillery, c.1795
This hired driver wears virtually civilian dress, with perhaps military gaiters (though civilian ones would be equally likely), with only the artillery hat identifying him as an army employee. Smocks varied in pattern, the quantity of stitched decoration depending upon personal taste.

B1: 'Battalion gunner', Buckinghamshire Militia, c.1794
This figure is taken from a rare depiction of a 'battalion gunner' by Capt. Sir William Young Bt. of the Buckinghamshire Militia, showing the battalion before the facings changed to blue in late 1794. The Buckinghamshire Militia was probably unique in retaining its battalion guns until they were handed over to the county yeomanry in 1816; the two brass 6-pdrs. had been purchased by public subscription in 1794. These accompanied the unit in the 1798 Irish rebellion and were even present on anti-riot duty in 1811/12.

B2: Artificer, Royal Military Artificers and Labourers, c.1795
The plates which accompany Connolly's regimental history appear in some cases to depict uniforms of a somewhat Victorian flavour; in particular, it is possible that the 'round hats' were squatter and narrower at the top than the Connolly plates suggest. This artificer wears ordinary uniform (not working dress) and carries a musket; in June 1792 it was requested that their bayonet scabbards be equipped with 'long brass chapes' as used by the 1st and 4th Bns., RA: the existing scabbards had button-ends which broke easily.

B3: Artificer, working dress, c.1795
This depicts the working dress of the Royal Military Artificers and Labourers, including a very plain jacket, one-piece 'gaiter-trousers' and a plain 'round hat' (for the shape of which, see Plate B2).

B4: Officer, Royal Artillery, c.1797
The uniform shown here evolved (as for the infantry) from the 18th-century style with open front, to that with lapels which buttoned over. For ordinary dress, this uniform was that worn virtually throughout the Napoleonic Wars, only changing

Royal Military Artificers, 1802: print after G. B. Campion from Connolly's *History of the Royal Sappers and Miners*. The uniform now resembles that of the infantry, with the shako adopted in 1802; blue jacket with black facings and yellow lace, white plumes (taller for the sergeant, centre) and white turnbacks. The sergeant has a crimson sash and carries the NCO's version of the 1796 infantry officers' sword, and a spontoon; the others have ordinary infantry equipment, which was later carried only by a minority of the corps.

with the introduction of the shako and short jacket in 1812, which probably took a couple of years to become universal.

C1: Corporal, Royal Artillery, c.1806
Based on Atkinson (but with a more likely arrangement of lace than the five breast-loops he shows), this figure wears the blue pantaloons and short gaiters which may have been used in walking-out dress, or may represent a difference in uniform between battalions of the Royal Artillery. The sword is the distinctive pattern which appears to have been introduced c.1800, and used until c.1816.

C2: Gunner, Royal Artillery, 1809
Based in part on Atkinson, this figure wears typical campaign dress of the earlier Peninsular War, with the breeches and gaiters which were commonly replaced by overalls during this period. The haversack and canteen were standard items carried on active service.

C3: Driver, Royal Artillery, c.1806
Taken from an illustration by J. A. Atkinson, this uniform depicts the dress of the Corps of Drivers

Royal Sappers and Miners, working dress, 1813: the short-tailed jacket without turnbacks. (Print after G. B. Campion from Connolly's *History of the Royal Sappers and Miners*.)

prior to the reintroduction of the 'Tarleton' helmet. The leather cap (perhaps worn concurrently with the 'Tarleton') may have been peaked, or with a folding peak; Atkinson shows one which appears to have no peak at all. The letters 'CD/RA' on the front represent 'Corps of Drivers, Royal Artillery'; possibly what is represented here is simply an undress uniform. Atkinson appears to show seven buttons in each of the three rows on the breast of the tailless blue jacket; modern reconstructions show many more buttons, but despite the fact that Atkinson shows the Foot Artillery with too few breast-loops, this version is more likely.

C4: 3rd Class Private, Royal Staff Corps, c.1810
This shows the uniform of the Staff Corps (also styled 'Staff Regiment of Infantry') prior to the adoption of a waist belt in place of one shoulder belt. The uniform is of infantry style, the facings and shoulder straps with the prescribed white piping, but no shoulder-tufts or lace loops on the cuffs or breast; because of this, the buttons may have been slightly larger than the usual pattern, those prescribed in 1817 having a leaf edge and bearing in the centre a crown over 'R.S.C.', with 'WATERLOO' above and 'PENINSULA' below; probably those used before had the same design but without the honours.

D1: Officer, Royal Engineers, c.1810

The original uniform of engineer officers, in the Ordnance colour of blue faced black, worn until the later stages of the Peninsular War, was easily confused; for example, at Badajoz Capt. Patten was mistaken by British sentries for a Frenchman when making a night reconnaissance. Buttons bore the Ordnance arms, and in 1796 it was ordered that officers carry the sword in a white shoulder belt, 'with an oval gilt plate, having the King's cypher with the crown over it, engraved in the centre'. Telescopes in leather cases were common.

D2: Private, Royal Military Artificers, c.1809

This depicts the likely appearance of the Artificers on landing in the Peninsula. Weaponry was varied; apparently those sent to Portugal carried only swords, whereas of those sent to Walcheren the youngest and most active had swords and the remainder muskets. Pikes and blunderbusses are mentioned for Peninsular detachments, and for many years the Gibraltar companies wore the accoutrements of a disbanded Newfoundland corps.

D3: Officer, Royal Waggon Train, c.1812

This figure is based on the Hamilton Smith plate, and upon an extant jacket with blue collar and cuffs and white turnbacks, the collar with two silver loops on each side, and six silver chevrons on each cuff. Similar chevrons were present on each short skirt, with four horizontal lines of lace joining the two buttons at the rear waist. The turnbacks were laced silver, bearing a double silver trefoil ornament on blue backing. The breast was profusely laced, with three rows of 25 buttons, the upper breast loop most unusually extending over the shoulder to a button at the top of the shoulder-blade, and running back at an acute angle to a button at the bottom of the collar, level with the rear end of the collar loops. The silver ball-buttons bore a crown over 'GR', with 'ROYAL WAGGON TRAIN' around the edge. Hamilton Smith shows the bicorn, but the shako was also worn with this uniform.

D4: Commissary

Being employees of the Treasury, commissaries had no regulated uniform, as different from the Quartermaster-General's department, which was a

Shown in the background of Hamilton Smith's plate of Quartermaster-Generals are two members of the Royal Staff Corps, wearing the 1812 shako (without cords), unlaced jackets, waist belts and blue pantaloons with short gaiters. On the left upper arm is the shield-shaped rank-badge which identified the grades of 1st and 2nd class private. (Aquatint by I. C. Stadler, from *Costume of the Army of the British Empire*, published January 1813.)

branch of the general staff and was uniformed accordingly. Many commissaries adopted quasi-military costume, including imitation uniforms ('an hermaphrodite scarlet coat' is one description!), and in this case a bicorn hat with foul-weather cover and a greatcoat of semi-civilian style as favoured by many army officers. No doubt some commissaries cultivated the facial 'whiskers' which at the time were indicative of a seasoned campaigner.

E1: Field Officer, Royal Artillery, 1814

This figure (from a contemporary picture) shows the 1812-pattern jacket with short tails and plastron lapels bearing gold loops, but unlike some fully-laced versions without the lace on the collar and turnbacks (doubtless many variations existed). The sabre is apparently a privately-chosen weapon, of which numerous patterns existed, brass or gilt stirrup hilts and scabbards being not unpopular.

Royal Sappers and Miners, 1813, showing the dress uniform with white breeches and black gaiters: print after G. B. Campion from Connolly's *History of the Royal Sappers and Miners*. Second left is apparently a sergeant major (with gold shoulder straps and lace, and a long-tailed coat); the seated figure is evidently an officer of the Royal Engineers. The large shako plate appears to be that worn on the earlier 'stovepipe' cap, conceivably added in error to the 1812 pattern in this (non-contemporary) illustration.

The horse-furniture is typical, the shabraque devoid of decoration save the tasselled rear corners, but the harness with metal fittings and plaited black fabric or leather decorations.

E2: Company Sergeant, Royal Artillery, 1814

This example of the 1812-pattern uniform illustrates the rank of company sergeant, which equated with infantry colour sergeants (which term was also used, unofficially, by the artillery). The first appointments were made in September 1813, but the rank badge is unclear; the regulation stated 'a Regimental colour above the chevrons, supported by two swords', but it is possible that infantry practice was copied, in a three-bar chevron on the left arm and the crowned flag and single chevron on the right. Drahonet's picture of Frederick Green-

wood in 1832 shows the crowned colour with swords at the bottom upon a three-bar chevron, which conforms to the 1813 description; so it is possible that this practice was always followed.

E3: Gunner, Royal Artillery, campaign dress, 1814

This 1812-pattern uniform includes the shako with waterproof cover (the plume with a cover also), as usually worn in service dress. The black knapsack is shown in contemporary sources with a variety of decoration: a red disc bearing yellow crown over 'R.A.'; with white or yellow letters 'R.A.' with or without a crown; Dighton (1813) shows a brown knapsack bearing yellow 'R.A.', and another in natural leather bearing crowned 'R.A.' in black. In light marching order the knapsack would be omitted and the rolled greatcoat slung across the back, as shown in another Dighton illustration.

F1: Officer, Royal Engineers, campaign dress, 1813

The scarlet Royal Engineers uniform adopted in 1812 is shown in contemporary pictures with partly turned-back lapels (as here), completely fastened over or showing a Garter-blue plastron with gold loops (the latter shown square-ended by Hamilton Smith but pointed elsewhere). How long the shoulder belt was worn is unknown, but it is not mentioned in the 1817 General Orders, which describe a waist belt upon which the honours 'Egypt' and 'Peninsula' might be worn by officers entitled to them.

F2: Corporal, Royal Sappers and Miners, 1813

As shown by Hamilton Smith, this represents the 1812-pattern infantry-style uniform, with a shako plate of the usual shape instead of the large plate shown (perhaps in error) by Connolly. Equipment remained much as before, with brass rectangular buckles instead of belt plates, though the Gibraltar companies apparently retained oval brass plates bearing the Ordnance arms, with 'GIBRALTAR' and 'SOLDIER ARTIFICERS' inscribed.

F3: Sergeant, Royal Sappers and Miners, working dress, 1813

Working dress consisted of a red jacket with short skirts but apparently no turnbacks, with blue facings and shoulder straps and small brass buttons (one on each rear cuff-seam); NCO chevrons were worn in yellow on the right arm only. The undress cap was black leather, with brass initials 'RS & M' worn on the front; an extant badge consists of a reversed royal cypher within a crowned strap inscribed 'ROYAL. REGt. OF. SAPPERS. AND. MINERS', conceivably for use on the same cap. Overalls were dark grey-blue with a reinforcement of the same material around the ankle, with red stripes and buttons on the outer seams, and short gaiters of similar colour. The companies at Cadiz are recorded as having overalls with a black stripe, and a grey cloth forage cap trimmed with black braid, bearing the brass initials on the left side.

F4: Private, Royal Sappers and Miners, working dress, 1813

When digging trenches it was usual for the men to work in single file, the leader 'breaking ground' and those behind deepening the trench progressively. To guard against the soil thus thrown around, the sappers improvised protective clothing which resembled that worn by civilian coal-heavers: blue-grey canvas 'breastplates' strapped around the wearer's back, and hoods of the same material,

folded and sewn at one end. The tools with which the sappers were issued were so inferior in quality that captured French tools were used whenever possible; as Wellington wrote, 'Is it not shameful that they should have better cutlery than we have?'

G1: Trooper, Mounted Rocket Corps, Royal Horse Artillery, 1814

Based upon Hamilton Smith's plate (published 2 January 1815), this shows the distinctive equipment of the Rocket Corps, the pistol holster on the waist belt and the pouch belt not normally used by the RHA. Congreve's book states that the sabre was carried on the saddle 'in action', 'that they may not be incumbered in mounting and dismounting', but this is not mentioned in Whinyates' correspondence with Siborne regarding the appearance of his troop at Waterloo. Whinyates urged Siborne not to show the small pennon attached to the rocket sticks,

The mounted version of the Royal Staff Corps was the Cavalry Staff Corps, whose uniform is shown by C. Hamilton Smith in a print from *Costume of the Army of the British Empire*, published 1 May 1813: red with blue facings and white lace, with a shako like that worn by the Royal Waggon Train post-1812. The letters on the valise, 'SD/A' signify 'Staff Dragoons, troop A'. (Aquatint by I. C. Stadler.)

A typical baggage-waggon: infantrymen with their families or camp-followers. (Print by W. H. Pyne, 1802.)

'added by the Captain as an ornament, and was discontinued, and not part of the real equipment'; but conceivably he wished it not to be shown simply because it was not an authorised item, not necessarily that it was not used at Waterloo. The presence of pennons would have fulfilled Congreve's intention that all rocket equipment be concealed under the shabraque, so 'that the Rocket trooper has merely the appearance of a lancer'.

G2: Corporal, Royal Horse Artillery, 1815

Taken from Dighton, this shows the rear lacing of the other ranks' jacket, and one variety of cuff-lace (another omits the trefoil knot). Rank distinctions were as for the Foot Artillery, but it is unclear when the chevrons became worn on both sleeves; some sources show the chevrons on the left arm only, and conceivably the practice varied between troops. This also illustrates the narrow black waterproof plume cover, and the sabre suspended from a shoulder belt instead of the waist belt used by some troops. Legwear also appears in various designs, this

example (after Dighton) having no leather reinforcing but two red stripes on the seams.

G3: Driver, Corps of Drivers, Royal Artillery, 1815

This depicts the Drivers' jacket resembling that of the Foot Artillery, plus bastion loop on the collar and with untufted shoulder straps. It is possible that this jacket was worn prior to that shown in Plate G4, but Vernet shows it worn by a mounted driver in an illustration dating from 1815 or later, apparently without the collar lace. Both Vernet and Sauerweid show curved sabres, doubtless of the 1796 light cavalry pattern, though conceivably drivers of Foot batteries might have carried the Foot Artillery sabre.

G4: Farrier, Corps of Drivers, 1815

The alternative Drivers' jacket is that shown by Hamilton Smith and Sauerweid, having three rows of buttons on the breast, surrounded by a 'frame' of yellow lace. (Sauerweid appears to indicate that the panels on which the buttons are set to be a darker shade than the remainder.) The fur cap, bearing a horseshoe badge, is a traditional pattern worn by cavalry farriers. Sauerweid shows overalls with two red stripes, whereas Vernet shows a single stripe set with a row of buttons.

H1: Quartermaster, Royal Horse Artillery, 1815

A contemporary portrait of Quartermaster James Wightman shows the uniform of a senior non-commissioned officer, including an officers'-style dolman with gold braid, crimson sash, and full dress white breeches. The shoulder decorations are perhaps unique to this rank; the shoulder belt appears to bear a brass or gilt plate, as shown by Hamilton Smith in his print of a gunner. The blue shabraque with tasselled end, and presumably a black sheepskin covering the saddle, are similar to those which appear to have been used by officers. The chinscales are fastened around the rear of the helmet; the badge consisted of the royal cypher within a crowned strap or garter, bearing the unit title or Garter motto.

H2: Officer, Royal Horse Artillery, 1815

This is based in part upon two portraits of Sir Augustus Frazer, one contemporary and one later than 1815, the former providing the pattern of the dolman (which in the later portrait has thicker braid). He wears a crimson hussar sash with gold barrels and tassel, and a pelisse, which in Frazer's case is shown with a fur lining, and black mohair braid but gold cords, though other portraits show black cords. The later Frazer portrait shows the pelisse worn over both shoulders like a cape, but others depict the more usual style, over the left shoulder.

H3: Assistant surgeon, infantry

This figure shows a uniform probably typical of infantry medical officers, the single-breasted medical coat but with regimental facings, lace and buttons. It is likely that some had the indented cuffs and buttons set vertically on the sleeve as worn by medical staff officers, but others seem to have had the collar and cuffs of their regiment. Supplies for immediate battlefield first aid would be carried in a satchel or haversack; the medical instruments (purchased personally by every surgeon) were generally carried in a sturdy wooden case.

* * *

Sources and Bibliography

For details of organisation, uniform and equipment, the following are of especial interest:
Services of the Royal Artillery in the Peninsular War (J. H. Leslie, London 1908–12); *Dress of the Royal Artillery* (D. A. Campbell, London 1971); *Wellington's Army in the Peninsula* (M. Glover, Newton Abbot 1977); *Wellington's Army* (H. C. B. Rogers, London 1979); *Peninsular Preparation* (R. Glover, Cambridge 1963); *British Military Uniforms 1768–96* (H. Strachan, London 1975); *History of the Uniforms of the British Army*, Vol. IV (C. C. P. Lawson, London 1966); *Details of the Rocket System* (Sir William Congreve, London 1814); *History of the Royal Sappers and Miners* (T. W. J. Connolly, 1855–57); *Weapons and Equipment of the Napoleonic Wars* (P. J. Haythornthwaite, Poole 1979); *The Royal Artillery Band* (H. G. Farmer, Journal of the Society for Army Historical Research Vol. XXIII, 1945, which updates the same author's *Memoirs of the Royal Artillery Band*, 1904); *Short Swords of the Foot Artillery* (A. W. Morrison & B. W. Reeder, *JSAHR* LVI, 1978).

Among the best contemporary accounts are:
Journal of the Waterloo Campaign (C. Mercer, Edinburgh & London 1870); *Letters written by Lt.Gen. Thomas Dyneley* (ed. F. A. Whinyates, Proceedings of the Royal Artillery Institution, London 1896); *An Engineer Officer under Wellington in the Peninsula* (R. Jones, ed. Hon. H. V. Shore, reprinted Cambridge 1986); *Diary of Campaigns in the Peninsula* (W. Swabey, reprinted London 1984).

Some of Mercer's and Robinson's comments are quoted in Campbell, above; extracts from Inspection Reports and orders are in Strachan, above.

Notes sur les planches en couleur

A1 D'après des portraits; notez en particulier le chapeau à bord rond que portent les officiers RA aux Pays-Bas, 1793–94, avec ici houppe de fourrure et cordons dorés. **A2** D'après Dayes—l'artilleur lorsque les Guerres Révolutionnaires éclatèrent. L'équipement de cuir blanc resta pratiquement tel quel jusqu'en 1815. **A3** Notez le chapeau à bord rond introduit (pour les artilleurs seulement) vers 1794 et nommé 'Mother Shipton', en référence à une célèbre sorcière! Les épaulettes jaunes marquent son rang. **A4** Un civil à la solde de Wellington, il porte peut-être des guêtres et un chapeau militaires, mais pas d'uniforme.

B1 Cette unité de milice a été unique pour avoir conservé ses 'canons de bataillon' jusqu'en 1816, les emportant lors de sa campagne en Irlande en 1798 et s'en servant pour supprimer des émeutiers en 1811–12. **B2** Uniforme quotidien ordinaire, et non pas tenue de corvée; les documents de source présentent un chapeau évoquant étrangement une forme victorienne qui a pu être plus carré et plus étroit qu'il n'est représenté. **B3** La tenue de corvée provient de la même source et les mêmes remarques s'appliquent au chapeau. **B4** Ce uniforme ordinaire d'un officier ne changeait guère pendant la guerre napoléonique, sauf que l'introduction d'un shako et une veste courte en 1812.

C1 Pantalons bleus et guêtres courtes qui auraient pu être la tenue de ville, ou autrement une tenue de campagne singulière à ce bataillon. Notez l'épée, utilisée vers 1800–16. Nous présentons des motifs de passement différents de ceux d'Atkinson sur la veste—ses cinq brandebourgs étant peu vraisemblables. **C2** Après Atkinson, l'uniforme porté était typique au commencement de la guerre d'Espagne, quoique en campagne on portait les pantalons habituellement. **C3** Le croquis par Atkinson n'est pas clair—le bonnet semble ne pas avoir de visière; et l'uniforme pourrait être une version de petite tenue. **C4** De style propre à l'infanterie, cet uniforme ne comportait ni brandebourgs ni houppes d'épaule, mais était garni d'un passepoil blanc.

D1 L'uniforme original de ce corps d'officiers qui fut souvent pris par mégarde pour des Français—avec des conséquences fatales. **D2** Les armes et les accoutrements provenaient de sources mixtes, avec piques et tromblons dans quelques unités. **D3** D'après une gravure d'Hamilton Smith et une veste qui a survécu. **D4** Ces civils adoptaient parfois un costume semi-militaire non réglementaire.

E1 Un tableau d'époque présente cette version, avec col et revers sans galons; de nombreuses variétés existaient sans nul doute. **E2** L'uniforme de 1812; dans le cas présent, un 'company sergeant', l'équivalent dans l'artillerie du nouveau grade de 'colour sergeant' dans l'infanterie. **E3** Modèle de 1812 d'uniforme de campagne, avec shako couvert. Des décorations variées de sac d'ordonnance sont présentées sur des gravures d'époque, portant généralement le monogramme 'RA' avec ou sans couronne.

F1 L'écarlate a été adopté en 1812 pour remplacer l'uniforme bleu. **F2** D'après une gravure d'Hamilton Smith, présentant un uniforme de modèle 1812 pour ce corps. **F3** Notez l'absence de rabats sur la veste; chevrons de grade sur le bras droit uniquement. **F4** Vêtement de cuir noir avec monogramme en laiton. **F4** Vêtement de protection improvisé pour travailler dans les tranchées. L'on préférait les outils français capturés à l'ennemi, considérés supérieurs à ceux de l'armée britannique.

G1 Hamilton Smith présente les articles distinctifs de ce corps comme un ceinturon avec étui de pistolet et ceinture à giberne. Le pennon sur les tiges de fusée était un apprêt de la 'Whinyates's Troop'. **G2** D'après Dighton, présentant une version du galon à l'arrière et sur le poignet; l'on ne sait pas clairement si les chevrons se portaient sur les deux manches, ou seulement sur celle de gauche. **G3** Une version, d'après Vernet; il est possible que ce type de veste ait précédé celle sur G4. **G4** Une alternative, d'après Hamilton Smith et Sauerweid; notez le bonnet traditionnel de maréchal-ferrant de la cavalerie.

H1 D'après un portrait d'époque de l'officier d'intendance James Wightman. **H2** D'après deux portraits de Sir Augustus Frazer. **H3** Probablement caractéristique des médecins du bataillon, cet uniforme se compose du manteau sans galon du corps médical mais avec parements régimentaires individuels. Les plumes étaient noires.

Farbtafeln

A1 Nach Portraits; siehe besonders den runden Hut der RA-Offiziere in den Niederlanden, 1793–94—hier mit Pelzverbrämung und Goldschnüren. **A2** Nach einem Bild von Dayes—ein Artillerist nach dem Ausbruch der Revolutionskriege. Die weisse Lederausrüstung blieb praktisch unverändert bis 1815. **A3** Siehe runden Hut, erstmals eingeführt etwa 1794 (nur für die Artillerie), genannt 'Mother Shipton' nach einer berühmten Hexe! Die gelben Epauletten geben den Rang an. **A4** Ein angeworbener Zivilist, trägt vielleicht Militärgamaschen und Hut, sonst aber nicht uniformiert.

B1 Diese Milizeinheit war wahrscheinlich die einzige, die ihre 'Bataillonskanonen' bis 1816 behielt, sogar im Einsatz in Irland im Jahre 1798, und bei Niederwerfung der Aufständischen 1811–12. **B2** Gewöhnliche Alltagsuniform, nicht Arbeitsuniform; die Quelle zeigt einen Hut von nahezu viktorianischer Form; er könnte eckiger und schmäler gewesen sein als hier gezeigt. **B3** Die Arbeitsuniform wurde derselben Quelle entnommen, ebenso wie der Hut. **B4** Die gewöhnliche Offiziersuniform änderte sich kaum während der napoleonischen Kriege, Ausnahmen sind das 'shako' und die kürzere Jacke.

C1 Blaue Pantalons und kurze Gamaschen könnten 'Ausgehuniform' gewesen sein, oder eine dem Bataillon eigentümliche Dienstuniform. Siehe Schwert, 1800–16. Wir zeigen andere Jackenschnürung als Atkinson—seien fünf Schlingen sind nicht überzeugend. **C2** Nach Atkinson diese Uniform war typisch am anfang der Peninsular krieg aber auf Feldzug waren Uniformhosen üblich. **C3** Atkinsons Zeichnung ist unklar—die Kappe scheint keinen Schirm zu haben, und es dürfte sich um eine Arbeitsuniform handeln. **C4** Diese Uniform im Infanterie-Stil hatte keine Schlingen oder Schulterverzierungen, war aber weissgerändert.

D1 Die Originaluniform für dieses ganz aus Offizieren bestehende Korps—sie wurden oft für Franzosen gehalten, mit unangenehmen Resultaten. **D2** Waffen und Ausrüstung stammten aus verschiedenen Quellen, und manche Einheiten hatten auch Piken und Blunderbusse. **D3** Nach einer Abbildung von Hamilton Smith; eine erhalten gebliebene Jacke. **D4** Diese Zivilisten trugen manchmal nicht-authorisierte halbmilitärische Kleidung.

E1 Ein zeitgenössisches Bild zeigt diese Version: unverschnürt am Kragen und am Revers. Zweifellos gab es viele Varianten davon. **E2** Die Uniform von 1812; in diesem Falle—ein Company Sergeant—das Artillerie-Äquivalent des neuen Ranges eines Colour Sergeant in der Infanterie. **E3** Uniform von 1812 für den Feldzug, mit bedecktem Tschako. Verschiedene Knapsack-Verzierungen sind auf zeitgenössischen Drucken zu sehen, meist mit dem Zeichen 'RA', mit oder ohne Krone.

F1 1812 wurde Schralachrot anstatt der blauen Uniform eingeführt. **F2** Nach Hamilton Smith's Abbildung—Uniform im Stil von 1812 für dieses Korps. **F** Siehe Fehlen von Jackenumschlägen; Rangabzeichen nur am rechten Ärmel schwarze Lederkappe mit Messingabzeichen. **F4** Improvisierte Schutzkleidung für die Arbeit in Schützengräben. Erbeutete französische Werkzeuge wurden bevorzugt—sie waren den britischen überlegen.

G1 Hamilton Smith zeigt als typische Merkmale für dieses Korps einen Gürtel mit Pistolenhalfter und einen Patronengurt. Der Wimpel an den Raketenstöcken war eine Eigenheit der Whinyate-Truppe. **G2** Nach Dighton—eine Version der hinteren und der Manschettenverschnürung; man weiss nicht ob Rangabzeichen auf beiden oder nur am linken Ärmel getragen wurden. **G3** Eine Version nach Vernet; diese Jacke ist möglicherweise älter als die von G4. **G4** Eine Alternativ nach Hamilton Smith und Sauerweid; siehe traditionelle Kavallerie Hufschmiedkappe.

H1 Nach einem zeitgenössischen gemälde von Quartermaster James Wightman **H2** Nach zwei Portraits von Sir Augustus Frazer. **H3** Wahrscheinlich typisch Regimentsärzte—diese Uniform hat den unverschnürten Mantel des medizinischen personals, aber ohne die individuellen Regimentsaufschläge. Die Feder waren schwarz.